crave

a passion for chocolate

crave
a passion for chocolate

Maureen McKeon

PHOTOGRAPHY BY ADRIAN LANDER

METRO BOOKS
NEW YORK

CONTENTS

INTRODUCTION

A passion for chocolate

Nothing stirs the senses like chocolate. The original soul food, it makes us feel good, appeals to the emotions, provides comfort and lifts the spirits. Certainly it is an absolute delight, and worthy of the passion people have felt for it over the centuries.

The secrets of chocolate have always fascinated me. My enduring love of chocolate began with my first bite of hedgehog, a confection that captured my childhood imagination with its enticing combination of broken sweet cookies, chopped walnuts and delicious chocolate. Sitting there in my aunt's rural kitchen, I was not to know that this would mark the beginning of a culinary career that would take me on journeys to places as diverse as little Mexican villages and sophisticated European capitals.

Chocolate can be as fancy or as simple as you like. Even a simple brownie or chocolate pound cake, when accompanied with ice cream or a fruit sauce and topped with chocolate curls and a sprinkling of confectioner's sugar, is transformed into a dessert as elegant as it is delicious. The flavors of fruits, nuts, and liqueurs marry perfectly with the superb richness of chocolate, creating endless possibilities for rich and delectable sweet treats.

For those who understand chocolate, working with it is a great joy, but for others, it can seem unnecessarily intimidating. This book aims to demystify cooking with chocolate. When basic techniques such as ganache and tempering are mastered, a world of creative possibilities opens up, with endless variations of inspiring textures, colors, and flavors. Working with chocolate inspires a new understanding of this wonderful food, and when given the right tools, even amateur cooks can achieve spectacular results.

I intend this book to educate the reader in all aspects of cooking with chocolate. I have been testing and developing chocolate recipes for many years; this is my passion and speciality, and my recipes are specifically tailored to ensure success for the novice as well as the experienced cook.

My son Andy is the one pushing for this book. He and his brother James grew up enjoying my chocolate treats, and for me, providing their young friends with recipes has been a very rewarding experience. Sharing the love of good food, especially chocolate, has been a great joy, and has inspired my wish to pass on my knowledge and enjoyment to others through this book.

chapter one

TECHNIQUES

There's nothing like baking to give a sense of satisfaction. The preparation and mixing, the anticipation while the cake cooks, the pleasure of decorating, and then eating it—each stage of the process has its own rewards. Baking and working with chocolate are often mistakenly regarded as tricky, but all that is required is a knowledge of chocolate's properties, and mastery of a few basic techniques.

UNDERSTANDING CHOCOLATE

Chocolate comes in various types, each with its own characteristics. It is not possible to make a great chocolate dish from inferior-quality chocolate, so always buy the best you can afford.

HOW CHOCOLATE IS MADE

Chocolate is produced from the fruit of the cacao bush, which is native to South America. The 'beans' from which chocolate is made grow in plump pods; once removed from the pods, the beans are fermented to develop their flavor, then sun-dried and shipped to factories for processing. There, they are roasted and broken into small 'nibs', which are then ground and refined; this is a lengthy and skilled process upon which the quality of the finished chocolate depends. The grinding process liquefies the cocoa nibs and removes some of the fat (also called cocoa butter) to produce a thick, dark, bitter paste known as cocoa liquor (or unsweetened, bitter or baking chocolate). This may then be further processed, with the addition of other ingredients—particularly sugar, milk solids or condensed milk—to produce the various types of chocolate.

A key stage in the production of chocolate is 'conching', a process of continuous stirring for several hours or up to three days. During conching, the chocolate is slightly heated to keep it liquid and to aid in the evaporation of excess moisture and volatile agents. This process is crucial to the smoothness and characteristic 'mouth feel' of chocolate; the longer it is conched, the better the finished product.

TYPES OF CHOCOLATE

The best types of chocolate for cooking are couverture, or the finest eating chocolates.

COUVERTURE A superior form of chocolate, couverture consists of at least 32 percent cocoa butter, plus cocoa liquor, and sugar (and, in the case of milk couverture, milk powder). The proportion of cocoa liquor to sugar is important; the higher the ratio of cocoa liquor, the darker and more bitter the chocolate.

Couverture has a rich flavor, a high sheen and a brittle texture, and is used in the making of chocolates and for the enrobing (or coating) of cookies, for dipping ice cream, and in the production of high-quality desserts. This is the chocolate that professionals use, but it is well suited to domestic use also, and is the recommended form of chocolate for all the recipes in this book. Dark, milk, and white couverture are available, in blocks of varying sizes or small chips known as callets.

DARK CHOCOLATE Dark chocolate contains 50–90 percent cocoa liquor, and no milk products. Those types with a higher percentage of cocoa liquor have very little sweetness; other types may have a balance of bitter and sweet due to the addition of sugar. The fat content varies, too; the higher it is, the better the chocolate melts in the mouth. Dark chocolate is the connoisseur's choice, and the type specified for most of the recipes in this book. Semisweet and bittersweet chocolate are both types of dark chocolate; which type you choose will depend on your palate.

MILK CHOCOLATE Milk chocolate contains cocoa butter, cocoa liquor, emulsifiers, sugar and milk powder. It should contain at least 25 percent dry cocoa solids. It is paler in color than dark chocolate, has a less intense flavor, and is sweeter. It can be substituted for dark chocolate in most recipes if it is more to your taste.

WHITE CHOCOLATE The product commonly known as white chocolate is not legally chocolate at all. The exception is white couverture, which by law must have a cocoa butter content of 32 percent. White chocolate (sometimes called 'white confectionery coating') contains cocoa butter, milk powder, sugar, and vanilla. Creamy-white and very sweet, it lacks the bitterness that cocoa liquor gives to other forms of chocolate.

White chocolate lacks a true 'chocolate' taste, but has a very creamy, melt-in-the-mouth texture. As it is not a true chocolate, it does not behave in the same ways as dark or milk chocolate, so cannot always be substituted for them in recipes.

COMPOUND CHOCOLATE In compound chocolate (also known as compound coating), cheaper vegetable oils replace some of the cocoa butter. This makes the product cheaper, more heat resistant and easier to use than true chocolate, and it does not require tempering. However, compound chocolate lacks the intensity of flavor and the luscious texture of true chocolate. In most cases it is best avoided. Compound chocolate must be labelled as such.

COCOA POWDER When chocolate liquor is partially defatted then pulverized, cocoa powder results. Dutch-process cocoa powder has been processed with an alkali to neutralize its natural acidity, reduce its bitterness and enhance its flavor. It is darker in color than natural cocoa powder (which has not been processed with an alkali) and has a milder chocolate flavor.

WORKING WITH CHOCOLATE

Chocolate is particularly sensitive to extremes of temperature and, when being melted, to the presence of water. When working with this most rewarding of foodstuffs, a little knowledge and some patience will ensure success.

STORING CHOCOLATE

Store chocolate in a cool place (approximately 64°F), but not in the refrigerator, as any moisture will alter the appearance of the chocolate. A 'bloom' (a grey, mottled cast) will develop on chocolate that has been exposed to high temperatures or to refrigeration or freezing. This is caused by the cocoa butter rising to the surface, and affects only the appearance of the chocolate, not its flavor or freshness.

Chocolate is very sensitive to odors, so take care to store it in a non-porous container away from strong-smelling foods.

GRATING CHOCOLATE

Chill for 10–15 minutes, then grate coarsely or finely using a box grater; or chop roughly using a heavy serrated knife, then grate in the food processor. Grating aids in melting, for example when making ganache or ice cream, especially when a small amount of liquid is being used.

MELTING CHOCOLATE

When melting chocolate on its own, remember these key points:
- use low temperature, as chocolate scorches easily;
- do not allow the chocolate to touch the heat source, as this causes graininess and caramelizes the chocolate;
- do not allow the chocolate to come into contact with water.

As chocolate is oil-based, even the tiniest droplet of water can cause chocolate to 'seize', or to form a thick, grainy mass that is unsuitable for use. Once this has happened, it is difficult to salvage, although the gradual addition of vegetable oil or melted vegetable shortening, stirring until smooth, may do the trick. Generally, if seizing occurs, you will need to start again with a new batch of chocolate. To avoid this happening, follow the method below, and make sure all utensils are clean and completely dry before you begin.

Unsweetened chocolate will liquefy when melted. Sweetened chocolate will hold its shape until stirred. All chocolate will continue to melt, and its temperature to rise, even after it is removed from a heat source, therefore care is needed to avoid overheating it.

There are two methods of melting chocolate: over a double boiler or in a microwave oven.

DOUBLE-BOILER METHOD
The ideal way to melt chocolate is in a bowl over a saucepan of hot water, or in the top of a double boiler.

1. To speed up the melting process, chop the chocolate with a heavy serrated knife; or chop roughly then grate in a food processor; or buy it as chips or callets.
2. Place the chocolate in a heatproof bowl that fits snugly over the saucepan.
3. Avoid covering the bowl with a lid, as this will cause steam to collect and fall as water droplets.
4. Fill the saucepan a quarter full of water and heat it almost to a boil.
5. Remove the saucepan from the heat and place the bowl of chocolate over it. It is vital that the water does not touch the bowl.
6. Gently stir the chocolate with a rubber spatula until smooth and liquid. Vigorous stirring will cause air bubbles to form, spoiling the finished product.
7. Should the water lose heat before the chocolate is fully melted, reheat the water, or tip it out and refill the bowl with hot water.

MICROWAVE METHOD
The microwave oven is a quick and efficient means of melting chocolate, so long as a few rules are followed.

1. Chop the chocolate with a heavy serrated knife; or chop roughly then grate in a food processor; or buy it as chips or callets.
2. Place the chocolate in a microwave-safe bowl.
3. Leave the bowl uncovered to prevent moisture from collecting.
4. It is important not to overheat the chocolate. For dark chocolate, heat on 50 percent, or medium power. For milk or white chocolate, use low power in 10-second intervals.
5. Stir gently with a rubber spatula after each burst of heating until the chocolate is melted.

Note that chocolate does not change its shape or melt in the traditional sense when heated in the microwave oven. It takes on a shiny appearance, but will retain its shape until stirred. How long the chocolate takes to melt will depend on the quantity of chocolate and the strength of the microwave oven. When in doubt, be cautious and use low power in short bursts.

MELTING CHOCOLATE WITH OTHER INGREDIENTS

Chocolate will seize if it comes into contact with a tiny amount of water, but paradoxically, it can be melted successfully with a larger amount of water, or with butter, or a mixture of both. Mixing chocolate and butter makes the chocolate smoother, subtler and more sensuous. The best chocolates and confectionery are determined by the quality and freshness of the butter as well as the quality of the chocolate. To melt chocolate with other ingredients:

1. Heat the water and/or butter over low heat. The water should be hot but not boiling, or the butter melted, before the chocolate is added.
2. Remove the saucepan from the heat and add the chopped or grated chocolate.
3. Allow to stand for a couple of minutes, then stir gently, using a rubber spatula, until the chocolate is melted and the mixture is smooth and well combined.
4. If adding sugar, do so once the chocolate and butter are combined, to prevent crystals from forming.

If a mixture of melted white chocolate and butter splits, refrigerate for a few minutes to cool it a little and bring it together.

TEMPERING CHOCOLATE

The purpose of tempering chocolate is to pre-crystallize the cocoa butter in the chocolate, thus ensuring the hardness and gloss of the finished product after it has cooled. During tempering, the cocoa butter changes into crystalline form, stabilizing the chocolate. If unstabilized through heating, these cocoa butter crystals can form a dull grey cast, or 'bloom', on the surface of the chocolate. Bloom also forms if chocolate is exposed to extremes of temperature, including refrigeration and exposure to direct sunlight. Chocolate affected by bloom is still fit to eat, and the bloom can be removed if the chocolate is retempered.

For most recipes in this book, it is not necessary to temper chocolate; tempering is mostly done when the chocolate will be used in confectionery or for decorations such as chocolate curls or cases. Commercially available chocolate is already 'in temper', but this changes when the chocolate is melted or exposed to extremes of temperature.

If the chocolate is melted in the normal way (to 40–45°C/ 104–113°F), then left to cool to working temperature, the finished product will not be glossy. If you make the effort of tempering the chocolate — that is, bringing it up to the right working temperature, so that there are sufficient stable crystals — you are guaranteed to get the desired result. The three factors that are important during tempering are time, temperature and movement.

A QUICK METHOD FOR TEMPERING CHOCOLATE

Very finely chop or grate the chocolate and set aside one-third of it in a covered container at room temperature, to prevent it from attracting moisture.

Melt the remainder in a heatproof bowl or the top of a double boiler over hot, but not simmering, water. Stir frequently with a rubber spatula to promote even melting. Test the chocolate with a sugar thermometer; the temperature should not exceed 45°C (113°F) for dark chocolate, or 40°C (104°F) for milk and white chocolate. Remove from the heat, then wipe dry the bowl or the top of the top boiler, to prevent any water from coming into contact with the chocolate. Stir in the reserved chocolate in three batches, allowing each to melt completely before adding the next. This will cool the chocolate to 26–28°C (79–82°F).

To rewarm the chocolate to working temperature, place the bowl or double boiler over warm, not simmering, water and warm again carefully, stirring until the correct temperature is obtained: 30–32°C (86–89.5°F) for dark chocolate, 29–31°C (84–88°F) for milk, and 29–30°C (84–86°F) for white.

Maintain the above working temperature during your working process. An appliance with an automatic temperature control is especially suitable for this purpose. Should the temperature exceed 32°C (89.5°F), begin over again with the tempering process.

OTHER INGREDIENTS USED IN BAKING

Few of the recipes in this book require unusual ingredients; most are store-cupboard staples.
As always with baking, buy the best ingredients you can afford.

BAKING POWDER This leavening agent is a combination of baking soda, an acid such as cream of tartar, and a moisture-absorbing agent such as cornstarch. When mixed with a liquid, the baking powder releases carbon dioxide gas bubbles, causing the cake or bread to rise. Baking powder is a dual-action leavener; it releases some gas when wet, and more when exposed to dry heat. It is perishable and should be kept in a cool, dry place. If unsure whether your baking powder is still viable, mix 1 teaspoon of it with 1/3 cup hot water. If it bubbles vigorously, it is fine to use.

BAKING SODA is sodium bicarbonate; used as a leavening agent. When combined with an acid liquid such as yogurt or buttermilk, baking soda produces carbon dioxide gas bubbles that cause the bread or cake to rise. Baking soda reacts immediately when moistened, so it should be mixed with the recipe's other dry ingredients before any liquid is added, then the mixture should be cooked at once.

BUTTER Use unsalted butter for baking, as it results in a sweeter, more tender crumb. Unsalted butter contains no preservatives, so it is more perishable than salted butter. Always use fresh butter, remembering that butter absorbs odors readily, and can easily become tainted if stored for too long or with strong-smelling foods.
Make sure the butter is at the right temperature. Chilled butter means butter straight from the refrigerator. Softened butter means butter returned to room temperature, which takes about 45 minutes.

CHEESE Various types of soft or fresh cheese are used in baking and for desserts.
Cream cheese This mildly tangy, spreadable cheese made from cow's milk and cream is an ingredient, along with cream or sour cream, in very rich cheesecakes.
Mascarpone cheese A rich, thick, mild-flavored Italian cheese made from cream to which citric or tartaric acid has been added.
Ricotta cheese Ricotta is made by heating whey and adding a coagulant; the resulting cheese is low in fat and can be used in cheesecakes and other desserts. Buy ricotta in bulk from a delicatessen; this form has a fresher flavor and better texture than the paste-like ricotta sold in tubs at supermarkets. Italian-style cheesecakes are usually made with sweetened ricotta, and are lighter than the American version.

COCOA In baking, it is preferable to use Dutch-process cocoa powder (see page 10) to give a good color and flavor.

CORN SYRUP This thick, sweet glucose syrup is made by processing cornstarch with acids or enzymes. Light corn syrup—the type called for in the recipes in this book—has been clarified to remove its color; dark corn syrup has a deeper color and tastes similar to molasses. It is used in such recipes as pecan pie, and in making frostings, and chocolate plastic.

CORNSTARCH A fine white powder milled from corn, used to thicken custards and in desserts. It contains no protein (gluten), unlike wheat flour. Used in combination with flour, it results in a lighter product, hence its inclusion in sponge cakes. It cannot be relied on alone as it contains no gluten.

CREAM Types of cream vary widely in fat content, and by name, between different countries. To avoid confusion, in this book we have specified if it is necessary to use whipping cream or heavy cream. Whipping cream, with a 30–36% fat content, is more forgiving than that with a higher percentage of fat, and is versatile; it can be used for both whipping and pouring. The majority of the recipes in this book use whipping cream.
Sour cream Traditionally made by allowing cream to naturally sour; today, cultured sour cream is made using pasteurized cream that is soured by adding a lactic-acid producing bacteria. To increase shelf life, it may be stabilized with additives such as gelatin.

CREAM OF TARTAR A fine white powder, originally derived from the crystals that are deposited on the inside of wine barrels; now often synthesized. A pinch of cream of tartar added to egg whites and sugar before beating them will help to stabilize the meringue. Cream of tartar is also a component in baking powder.

EGGS Large (2 1/2 oz) eggs have been used in all recipes in this book. Always use eggs at room temperature for better volume and to enable better mixing and incorporation in cake mixtures. Egg whites, too, should always be used at room temperature for the best volume. For eggs to attain room temperature, remove them from the refrigerator about 45 minutes before using them.

FLOUR All grains, and some nuts and legumes, can be ground into flour, but the term 'flour' generally refers to wheat flour. Wheat flour contains a protein called gluten, which, when combined with a liquid, forms the elastic network that helps contain the gases that make mixtures such as cakes and breads rise as they bake. Gluten can be developed by mixing and kneading; this is desirable in bread (which is why bread mixtures are kneaded) but not in cakes. Unless otherwise instructed, cake mixtures should be mixed lightly until all the ingredients are just combined, to ensure a tender result.

All-purpose flour is a multi-purpose flour that can be used for cakes, pastries and breads. When used in cakes, a leavening agent such as baking powder or baking soda is usually added to it.

Self-rising flour has baking soda and salt added to leaven it.

GELATIN A colorless, almost flavorless protein used as a setting agent, mainly for desserts. Although recipes will give an exact amount of gelatin required, the resulting set will vary according to the brand and what you are setting. If gelatin is boiled or if acidic liquids are added to it, it may lose its setting qualities, and some fruits (such as pineapple, papaya and figs) contain enzymes that will eat the protein in gelatin and will not allow it to set. Gelatin is sold in powdered form and as clear leaves. Generally 3 teaspoons or 6 sheets will set 2 cups of liquid.

- Using powdered gelatin: Put 3 tablespoons water into a glass bowl and sprinkle on the gelatin evenly. Leave the gelatin to 'sponge', or swell. Add the sponged gelatin to a hot liquid and stir well to dissolve it.
- Using leaf gelatin: Soak the gelatin sheets in cold water for 1 minute, or until they are floppy. Squeeze out any excess water, and then stir the sheets straight into a hot liquid to dissolve them.

GLYCERINE Glycerine (chemically, an alcohol) is the commercial name for glycerol, an odorless, colorless, syrupy liquid obtained from fats and oils and used to retain moisture and add sweetness to foods. It also helps to prevent the crystallization of sugar in candies. Add a few drops of glycerine to ganache to add shine, or to glacé frostings to prevent them from crystallizing.

HONEY The color, flavor and aroma of honey depend on the type of flower from which the nectar is taken. Blended honeys—those made from several different types of flowers—are good all-purpose honeys suitable for baking. Flower honeys—those made from one particular type of flower—are best reserved for eating.

Honey is an invert sugar, which means that if you add a little to sugar syrup or caramel, it will stop their sugars from crystallizing.

LEAVENING AGENTS Also known as raising agents, these are used to lighten the texture and increase the volume of cakes, breads and cookies. There are two types: natural (egg whites and yeast) and chemical (baking soda and cream of tartar).

Egg whites When beaten egg whites are added to, for example, a cake mixture then baked, the egg white cooks and sets, trapping the air inside and resulting in a light, airy cake. This is the form of leavening that is used in sponge cakes and chiffon cakes.

Yeast Living, single-celled fungi that feed on carbohydrates, breathe air and give off carbon dioxide and alcohol. When used in baking, yeast converts the natural sugars in the flour to bubbles of carbon dioxide. These are trapped by the elastic network formed by the gluten in the flour, stretching it as they expand, thus giving bread its texture. Baking kills the yeast and sets the dough.

Yeast needs warmth and moisture to thrive, which is why it is usually mixed with a warm liquid before being added to the dry ingredients in a recipe. Fresh yeast is sold as a compressed solid and can be stored in the refrigerator for up to 1 week, or frozen for several months (it will reactivate when exposed to warmth and moisture). Dried yeast will keep for up to 1 year in a cool, dry place.

Chemical leavening agents These work by creating carbon dioxide gas bubbles when mixed with water; the bubbles cause a mixture or dough to rise during baking. See also Baking powder, Baking soda and Cream of tartar (page 15).

LIQUEURS Alcoholic syrups distilled from wine or brandy and flavored with fruit, herbs, or spices. In baking or sauces, they can usually be replaced by the same quantity of a similarly flavored liquid, or omitted entirely, with little detriment to the recipe.

NUTS As well as adding delicious flavor, nuts add texture to cakes and cookies. Ground nuts may also provide body in some flourless cakes. To toast nuts, put them in a single layer on a baking tray and bake in a preheated 350°F oven for 5–10 minutes. Stir occasionally with a wooden spoon to aid even toasting, and keep an eye on them, as they can burn easily.

SPICES Spices are aromatic seasonings obtained from plants. They include seed pods, seeds, stems, bark, roots, buds, berries, and fruits. They should be used sparingly so as not to dominate or overpower the other flavors in the dish. Ground spices lose their flavor and aroma quickly, so buy them in small quantities and store in an airtight container in a cool, dark place for up to 6 months only. Where possible, buy whole spices and grind them as needed using a spice grinder or mortar and pestle.

SUGAR Mostly produced from sugar cane; it can also come from sugar beet (both sugars taste the same). Other sources are honey, sorghum, palm trees and maple trees. Both granulated sugars and cane sugar syrups are used in baking; the most common types are:

Brown sugar Originally, a partly refined sugar flavored with the molasses from which it was made; now also made by adding molasses to white sugar. Types include Barbados (muscovado) sugar, a light or dark, strongly flavored sugar; light soft brown sugar, with a light, fine grain and a caramel sugar flavor; and dark soft brown sugar, which is moist and has a molasses flavor. For chocolate chip cookies, brown sugar is used, as it helps to preserve the shape of the chocolate chips during baking.

Cane sugar syrups These are by-products of sugar refining.
- Treacle has a strong, slightly bitter flavor and adds richness and color to baked goods.
- Light treacle is an invert sugar syrup (meaning it won't crystallize) with a honey-like texture and a distinctive, rich flavor. It can be used in baking or as a pouring syrup.

Confectioner's sugar Made by grinding granulated sugar to a fine powder, which dissolves instantly. It is used for frostings, to sweeten whipped cream and to dust over cakes and desserts for decoration. There are two types:
- Pure confectioner's sugar, the type usually called for in this book, has no additives and tends to be quite lumpy; it will need to be sifted before use. Any very large lumps can be broken up in a food processor before sifting.
- Confectioner's sugar mixture contains cornstarch as an anti-caking agent.

Granulated sugar A bleached sugar refined from cane sugar or sugar beet, this is the most common, all-purpose sugar and is referred to in this book simply as 'sugar'. The crystals do not dissolve as easily as those of superfine sugar.

Maple syrup The sap of the maple tree, boiled until much of the water has evaporated and it is thick and syrupy. As its production is labor intensive, pure maple syrup is costly. Imitations labelled 'maple-flavored syrup' are available; they are cheaper than pure maple syrup, but their flavor is inferior.

Superfine sugar A fine, white sugar with very small crystals that dissolve easily.

SUGAR SYRUP A mixture of sugar and water (sometimes flavored with alcohol), boiled then cooled and used to brush on cakes to moisten them, add flavor and to help frostings adhere to the surface.

VANILLA True vanilla comes from the pod of a climbing orchid vine native to Central America. The pods are sun-dried, causing them to shrivel, turn deep brown and develop a light coating of white vanillin crystals. True vanilla is expensive due to the labor-intensive methods of obtaining it, and is sold in either pods or distilled into pure vanilla extract. Good-quality vanilla pods have a warm aroma, and should be soft and flexible, not hard and dry. The pod (whole or halved) can be infused in hot milk to use in ice cream or custard. For extra flavor, the tiny, intensely flavored seeds can be added. Vanilla pods can be used up to four times before they lose their flavor; after use, wash, dry thoroughly and store, wrapped in plastic, in a cool, dry place.

Synthetic or imitation vanilla flavoring, which must be labelled as such, is less expensive but has an inferior flavor. For best results, always use pure vanilla.

YEAST See Leavening agents (opposite).

EQUIPMENT

A surprisingly small range of bakeware and other equipment will see you through most baking recipes. Invest in good-quality items, such as those from a professional catering store; if properly cared for, they should last you for life.

When choosing cake pans and baking trays, avoid dark non-stick finishes, as they tend to result in overcooked products. Select durable aluminum pans and baking trays for the best baked results. Buy pans with welded, non-leaking seams.

When choosing other equipment, remember that plastic, rubber and wood absorb strong odors, as does chocolate. To avoid odors from other foods tainting your cakes and desserts, it is a good idea to have two of such utensils as wooden spoons and rubber spatulas, reserving one for savory foods only and one for sweet mixtures.

BAKEWARE

CAKE PANS There are myriad sizes and shapes of cake pans, but the following is a good basic selection.

Round cake pans
- Two 8 inch diameter
- Two 9 inch diameter
- Two 10 inch diameter

Square cake pans
- One 7 inch
- One 8 inch
- One 9 inch

Springform pans Used for baking cheesecakes and fragile cakes, as the spring clip can be unbuckled and the side of the pan gently eased away from the cake.
- One 9 inch diameter
- One 10 inch diameter

Loaf pan
- one 9 x 5 x 3 inches deep

Shallow rectangular pan
- one 13 x 9 x 2 inches deep

A selection of molds, such as gugelhopf molds and ring pans, and muffin pans of various capacities.

BAKING SHEETS When making cookies and some pastries, baking sheets sheets or cookie sheets are required. The best are the flat sheets with either one or both ends turned up. The flat sides enable the baked goods to be slid off the tray easily. Buy at least two sheets, or more if you have enough oven racks to hold them. They should be heavy, so that they will heat evenly and not warp.

BAKING DISHES A selection of glass or ceramic ramekins, baking dishes and soufflé dishes in various sizes can be used for baked or chilled desserts.

SUBSTITUTING CAKE PANS If you don't have the specified pan size or shape, you can substitute by making an adjustment of about 3/4 inch between a round and a square pan; for example, an 8 inch round pan and a 7 inch square pan have a similar capacity.

MEASURING EQUIPMENT

MEASURING CUPS AND SPOONS Stainless steel cups and spoons are preferable to plastic. You will need 1/4 cup, 1/3 cup, 1/2 cup and 1 cup sizes in measuring cups. Measuring spoons come as a set: 1 tablespoon, 1 teaspoon, 1/2 teaspoon and 1/4 teaspoon. We have used a 1/2 fl oz tablespoon measure throughout for all recipes.

MEASURING JUG Use a heatproof glass jug to measure liquids.

WEIGHING SCALES Baking is a precise science, so invest in an accurate set of scales to ensure best results. Electronic scales are the most accurate. Balance scales also work well but must be able to be accurate to as little as 1/8 oz.

MIXING EQUIPMENT

ELECTRIC MIXER If you can afford it, buy a heavy-duty stand mixer in preference to a hand-held mixer; stand mixers are stronger, come with more attachments (for kneading bread dough, for example) and will give you a more professional result. Purchase an extra bowl if possible, and select stainless steel over plastic bowls.

FOOD PROCESSOR These time-saving machines are good for making simple batters and cake mixes, and are ideal for grinding nuts and chopping or grating chocolate.

MIXING BOWLS It is useful to have a set each of glass and metal mixing bowls. Stainless-steels bowls conduct heat well and are ideal for melting chocolate or other ingredients over a saucepan of hot water. Glass or ceramic bowls are best for beating egg whites and for general mixing purposes. Plastic bowls are not recommended, as they absorb odors and also tend to retain grease, which can cause egg whites to fail to attain maximum volume when beaten.

RUBBER SPATULA For stirring, folding and levelling mixtures and for scraping cake mixtures out of the mixing bowl.

SPOONS Wooden spoons are essential items used for blending mixtures and for stirring. They do not scratch saucepans or conduct heat. They do, however, absorb odors, so keep separate wooden spoons for sweet and savory recipes. Large metal spoons are best for folding in dry ingredients, as their sharp edges cut easily through the mixture without causing it to lose too much air.

WHISK A balloon whisk is useful for whisking egg whites, smaller quantities of cream, and delicate fillings that can easily be over-whisked if using an electric mixer. Various sizes are available.

OTHER EQUIPMENT

CAKE TESTER A long, thin, purpose-built metal skewer with a sharp pointed end, used to test a cake to see if it is baked. A wooden skewer or toothpick will also do the job.

DIGITAL PROBE THERMOMETER For monitoring the heat of delicate mixtures and for the tempering of chocolate.

KNIVES Buy the very best you can afford. Start with a small vegetable knife, a cook's knife and a serrated bread knife for slicing cakes when serving them. A thin-bladed ham knife is useful for slicing cakes horizontally before filling them.

OVEN THERMOMETER These are designed to stand or hang in the oven. When baking, it is vital to check that the oven temperature is accurate, as the calibration of inbuilt oven thermometers can slip in accuracy over time.

PALETTE KNIFE A long, thin-bladed metal spatula with a rounded end, ideal for transferring cookies from their baking sheet to a wire rack, and for spreading fillings and frostings.

PARCHMENT PAPER A non-stick paper formulated specially for baking; used to line cake pans and baking sheets. It is much used by professional chefs.

PASTRY BRUSH For buttering cake pans, glazing bread and pastry doughs and sealing pastry pie dough. A brush with natural bristles is best; nylon bristles may melt when used with hot liquids.

ROLLING PIN For rolling out pastry and for crushing cookies or nuts. A long wooden rolling pin, about 19 inches long and 1½ inches in diameter, is the best all-round pin. A pin of this size is large enough to roll out an entire sheet of pastry at once, making it easier to control the thickness of the pastry. Wood is preferable to ceramic or marble as its surface collects and holds a fine layer of flour, making the pastry less likely to stick to it.

SIEVE Buy a large sieve for sifting dry ingredients, and a smaller one for dusting baked goods with confectioner's sugar or unsweetened cocoa powder. Buy a sieve that has a lip so it can rest on the edge of the bowl. Stainless-steel mesh lasts longer than plastic.

SUGAR THERMOMETER For making caramel and for candy making.

WIRE RACK These may be round, square or rectangular. They are essential for cooling baked items; the metal grids enable air to circulate around the food during cooling, preventing steam from building up underneath it and making it soggy. Various grades of mesh are available; a rack with fine mesh will leave a less obvious pattern on the surface of the cake.

TECHNIQUES AND TIPS FOR SUCCESSFUL BAKING

Baking is a little like kitchen alchemy; from a few basic ingredients come enticing results that give a sense of satisfaction out of all proportion to the effort needed to achieve them.

BEFORE YOU BEGIN

READ A RECIPE THOROUGHLY BEFORE YOU START
If you don't have an ingredient, use a suitable substitute. In many of the recipes, a variation is suggested, but you can try your own variations. Gather together all the ingredients for efficient working. It is a good idea to test drive a recipe before preparing it for guests. This allows you to make adjustments for your own oven, as all ovens differ slightly in how long they take to cook dishes.

PREPARING THE OVEN
Check the position of the oven racks. In gas ovens, the top rack is the hottest. In an electric oven, bake on the middle shelf or the next one down. Always pre-heat the oven at least 10 minutes before using (longer if your oven is wider than standard). The recipes in this book have been written for a regular oven; if using a fan-forced oven, reduce the temperature by about 35°F.

PREPARING THE BAKING EQUIPMENT
For cakes Prepare the cake pans, and check you have all other necessary equipment, before you commence baking.

Use the size of cake pan specified in the recipe. To check the diameter of a cake pan, measure across the top from inside edge to inside edge.

Some recipes will call for the cake pan to be buttered and floured; be sure to turn the pan upside down and tap out excess flour. Other recipes will specify that the pan be buttered then lined with parchment paper. A second buttering is optional. Use freshly melted butter and a pastry brush. After preparing the pans, put them in the refrigerator while preparing the recipe. This will ensure that the coating stays intact.

To flour a cake pan when making a chocolate cake, use equal amounts of unsweetened cocoa powder and flour sifted together; this will give a darker appearance to the finished cake than the use of flour alone. Sprinkle a small amount into the pan and rotate it so that the whole inner surface is evenly covered. Tap the pan to remove excess.

For cookies When making cookies, prepare baking sheets as specified. Not all recipes require the sheet to be buttered or lined. If the recipe does specify to butter the baking sheet, do so lightly; the aim is to prevent them from sticking, not to fry them. Too generous a layer of butter will cause the cookies to spread too much.

For custards and desserts For making desserts, butter the dish beforehand. This step is not necessary for custards, including crème brûlée and crème caramel.

MEASURING AND SIFTING

MEASURING INGREDIENTS ACCURATELY
Stick to one system of measurement (cups) rather than mixing different systems. Use scales, measuring cups, and measuring spoons. Spoon dry ingredients into a measuring cup or spoon and level the surface with the back of a knife.

It is important to note that scooping a dry ingredient such as flour out of the packet using a measuring cup will cause the ingredient to pack down, giving a greater weight than if it is spooned into a cup. For this reason, it is best to spoon out the dry ingredients to avoid an inaccurate measurement. All cup and spoon measurements are level unless otherwise stated. Measure liquids in calibrated jugs on a flat surface at eye level.

SIFTING DRY INGREDIENTS
Sift ingredients using a medium-gauge stainless-steel sieve. Do this before you commence preparation, then again at the point of addition; this gives a lighter batter. For the second sifting, sift the dry ingredients onto a sheet of parchment paper, from which they can be poured easily into the mixture.

MIXING
How a cake should be mixed depends on the method of making it. There are three main methods for making cakes, each of which produces a cake with a different texture. Cakes with a base of creamed butter and sugar have a short, soft crumb due to their high percentage of fat. Whisked cakes are made with plenty of eggs, which aerate the batter. These cakes tend to rise dramatically in the oven, then fall back a little once cooked, although their texture remains light and fluffy. Cakes made using the melt-and-mix method, in which the butter and sugar are melted together, have a particularly moist, dense crumb and good keeping qualities.

In a mixture that has a base of creamed butter and sugar or whisked eggs, the dry ingredients are generally mixed in by hand

to give a lighter texture. In a mixture with a melted butter base, however, the dry ingredients are sometimes beaten in with an electric mixer. The method of beating will greatly influence the texture of the finished cake, so follow the recipe's instructions.

Unless otherwise instructed, cookie doughs and pastry should also be mixed only until the ingredients are just combined; overmixing may result in a tough product.

If you are having trouble getting a cake mixture to combine—for example, if you are working with a deep mixing bowl—you may find it helpful to transfer the mixture from one bowl to another. This ensures the batter is thoroughly mixed.

BEATING EGG WHITES

Beating egg whites to the right stage is crucial. A reference to 'soft-peak' stage means that when the beaters are lifted, the egg whites should just hold their shape. 'Firm-peak' stage means that the egg whites hold their shape firmly when the beaters are lifted. These stages are particularly important in meringue making (see also page 26). Note that overbeating causes loss of volume and makes the egg whites difficult to fold into the rest of the mixture.

CREAMING BUTTER AND SUGAR

Use butter that has been brought to room temperature; this is what is meant by softened butter. It takes about 45 minutes for chilled butter to return to room temperature. It should still hold its shape, and not be runny or oily. Using an electric mixer, beat on medium speed until the butter is of an evenly creamy consistency, then add the sugar and continue beating on medium–high speed until the mixture is pale and fluffy, and drops easily from the beaters. The time this takes will depend on the quantity being beaten.

In dire straits, butter can be softened in the microwave, although this method requires vigilance and careful timing! For a 9 oz block, microwave on the lowest setting for about 30 seconds, then test, remembering that the center will be softer than the outside. If it requires further softening, do so in 10-second bursts.

BEATING OTHER INGREDIENTS

If adding eggs to a creamed butter and sugar mixture, do so carefully and gradually or the mixture may begin to separate. Add whole eggs one at a time, or beaten egg about 1 tablespoon at a time, beating well after each addition before adding any more. Using a rubber spatula, scrape the bowl and beaters well between additions. If the mixture separates, all is not lost; beat in a tablespoon or so of the flour from the recipe, then continue carefully adding the eggs.

FOLDING

Folding is the term used to describe a very light type of mixing, typically done to incorporate beaten egg whites into another mixture without decreasing their volume. The mixture is scooped gently and slowly up from the bottom of the bowl, then the bowl is turned slightly and the process is repeated until the two mixtures are combined. Folding is best done with a large metal spoon, or sometimes with a rubber spatula, the sharp edges of which will cut through the mixture without deflating the egg whites too much.

ROLLING OUT DOUGHS

When rolling out pastry or cookie dough, place the ball of dough on the work surface, flatten it slightly with your hand, then roll from the center out in one direction then another. Do not roll the rolling pin back and forth, as this causes the pastry to stretch too much and then shrink back when baked. Avoid flattening the edges of the dough by rolling the pin over them and onto the work surface; the aim is to have an even thickness overall.

FILLING CAKE PANS AND PLACING COOKIES ON TRAYS

Cakes and bar cookies When making cakes, fill the pans no more than half full, to allow for rising during baking. Cheesecakes are an exception; these should be filled almost to the top unless the recipe states otherwise.

Bar cookies do not generally contain much leavening agent, and thus they rise little, if at all, so the pans can be filled closer to the top.

Cookies Cookies spread during baking, some more than others. Most average-sized baking sheets fit three rows of four cookies, with the cookie mixture spaced about 2 inches apart. To prevent excessive spreading, some recipes may call for the mounds or pieces of cookie mixture to be chilled or frozen on their sheets for 30 minutes or so before baking.

If using a cookie cutter to stamp out cookie shapes, dip the cutting edge into a little extra flour from time to time to prevent it from sticking.

DURING AND AFTER BAKING

TIMING

Use a timer for cooking accuracy so that you don't forget the cooking time and need to guess. If a range of cooking times is given, for example 50–60 minutes, test the cake after 50 minutes then continue cooking if need be. Remember that cooking times are a guide only; individual ovens vary considerably in how long they take to cook items. Always be guided by how the cake looks when tested rather than by a given cooking time.

Most ovens are not equally hot in each part of their interior; the bottom may be hotter than the top, or the front hotter than the back, for instance. Unless cooking a sponge cake, which must remain undisturbed, turn the cake or other baked item(s) around halfway through baking to ensure even cooking. If cooking two cakes or two sheets of cookies, swap them between the oven shelves also.

If a cake begins to brown too much on top before it is cooked through, cover it loosely with a sheet of foil.

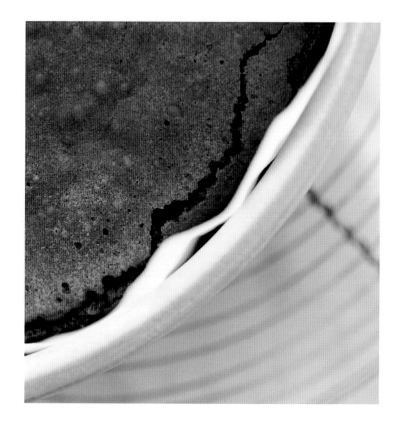

TESTING WHETHER BAKED GOODS ARE COOKED

Cakes There are several ways of judging whether a cake is cooked: when it starts to shrink back slightly from the edge of the pan; when it springs back when pressed lightly in the center with a finger; or when a skewer inserted into the center of the cake comes out clean. If there is any sticky cake mixture left on the skewer, return the cake to the oven and cook for 5 minutes more before retesting. This process can be repeated until the skewer comes out clean.

Note that with cakes that contain a lot of fruit or a large amount of chocolate, or those that are meant to have a sticky texture, the skewer will not come out entirely clean. To test these cakes, run your finger along the skewer after testing to check for moisture. If the mixture is wet, the cake is not ready; however, if the mixture holds its shape, the cake is cooked.

Cookies Pale-colored cookies—that is, those that do not contain chocolate or cocoa—should be cooked until they are dry on top, and are pale golden in color on both top and bottom. Use a palette knife or metal spatula to lift a cookie from the sheet to check the bottom. Some types of cookies will crack on top, another indication that they are cooked. To test cookies containing cocoa or chocolate, towards the end of the cooking time, lift one cookie off the tray and check its underside. If there is a darker, damp-looking patch in the center, the cookies are not yet cooked.

If the cookies are undercooked, cook for just 2 minutes more, then retest. Always keep a good check on them, as cookies can be underdone one minute and burnt the next.

COOLING BAKED GOODS

Cool baked cakes in their pans on a wire rack for 10 minutes, or the time specified, then loosen the edge using a small metal spatula and turn the cake out onto a wire rack (or, if using a springform pan, remove the outer ring). Remove the parchment paper from the bottom and sides of the cake while it is still warm. If you don't want rack marks on the top of the cake, invert it so that it is right side up. Allow the cake to cool completely on a wire rack before filling and frosting it. Some cakes with a very delicate or moist texture may need to be cooled completely in the pan before removal.

When making cookies, the same sheet (and the same sheet of parchment paper) can be used for more than one batch, but the sheet must be allowed to cool before the new batch is put onto it, otherwise the cookies may spread too much.

CLEANING AND CARING FOR BAKEWARE

Wash cake pans and baking sheets in hot soapy water, rinse well and dry thoroughly. Pans can be further dried in a still-warm oven once your cooking session is finished. Non-stick pans should not be washed; simply wipe them out with paper towels.

Never put hot cake pans or baking sheets in hot or cold water, as this will distort the shape. Always allow cake pans to cool completely before washing them.

Avoid putting hot glass or ceramic baking dishes into cold water, as this may cause them to crack. Allow to cool, then, if necessary, fill with water to assist in softening any burnt-on mixture.

STORING BAKED GOODS

Cakes

- Allow unfrosted cakes to cool completely before storing, or they will become sticky.
- Cakes with creamy frosting should be stored at room temperature in a cake box or under a cake dome.
- Cakes made with whipped cream, mousses or cheese frostings should be refrigerated in a covered container.
- Avoid using plastic wrap to cover frosted cakes, as it will mark the surface.
- Chocolate cakes should be stored at room temperature, unless they contain cream fillings; refrigeration will dry out the cake and diminish its flavor, as well as spoiling the appearance of a ganache frosting.
- Most cakes, if unfrosted and well wrapped, can be frozen for up to 6 months. Thaw first in the refrigerator, then at room temperature to prevent condensation from developing.

Cookies and bar cookies

- Allow to cool completely, then store in an airtight container. If making more than one type of cookie or bar cookie, store each in a separate container. Note that leaving crisp cookies on the rack for too long on a very humid day may cause them to absorb moisture and become soft.
- Layers of frosted cookies or bar cookies can be separated by parchment paper to prevent the frosting from sticking.
- If cookies become soft during storage, put them on a baking sheet in a moderate oven for a few minutes to re-crisp them.

Pastry

- Uncooked pastry should be refrigerated until needed. It may be frozen; when needed, leave at room temperature to allow it to soften to a rolling consistency.
- When storing cooked pastry goods, store in an airtight container at room temperature; do not refrigerate, or the pastry will become soft.
- Cooked pastry may be rewarmed in a moderate oven for a few minutes if desired.
- Pastry should not be reheated in a microwave oven, as it will become tough and soggy.

SLICING AND SERVING

Slicing cakes into layers before filling To create even layers, use a ruler and toothpicks to mark the cake vertically into equal divisions. Repeat around the cake at intervals. Using a long sharp knife, and following the lines of toothpicks to guide you, slice the cake into even layers, rotating the cake as you cut.

Slicing cakes for serving The best type of knife to use when slicing cakes for serving depends on the kind of cake and its filling.

- To slice chocolate cakes, cheesecakes, and other sticky or dense cakes for serving, dip a cook's knife in hot water, wipe it dry, then slice; repeat after each slice to prevent the cake from sticking to the knife.
- For delicate and sponge cakes, use a serrated knife.
- For other cakes, use a serrated knife or a cook's knife.
- For cakes with creamy or messy fillings, use a cook's knife.
- If dusting with confectioner's sugar, do so just before serving, as the confectioner's sugar will eventually absorb humidity in the air, spoiling its delicate, powdery effect.

TIPS FOR WORKING WITH VARIOUS MIXTURES

*When preparing meringues, soufflés, sponge cakes and pastry,
follow these hints to make the process easier and ensure success.*

MERINGUE

It is critical that the egg whites be completely free from egg yolk and that the bowl and whisk or electric beaters are spotlessly clean and completely dry. The smallest amount of grease or butter will reduce the ability of the egg white to 'foam'.

Commence beating on a medium speed then increase to a high speed. Don't overwhip egg whites, as the protein separates out, leaving clumps and liquid. Stir to loosen the mixture before adding other ingredients. Add sugar gradually to beaten egg whites, a tablespoon at a time, beating between additions to allow the sugar to dissolve.

To add stiffly beaten egg whites to a mixture, gently fold in one-third of the egg whites, thus lightening the mixture, then fold in the remaining egg whites.

SOUFFLÉS

Prepare the molds or ramekins by buttering well. Dust the insides with confectioner's sugar, tapping out any excess. This enables the mixture to cling to the side of the dish as the mixture rises during baking.

SPONGE MAKING

The mixing bowl must be scrupulously clean; also, stainless steel gives a better aeration than plastic. Use a wire whisk attachment if your mixer has one. Add the sugar to the eggs and whisk on high speed to achieve maximum volume, then reduce the speed to medium to stabilize the air bubbles.

Dry ingredients should be sifted twice to ensure a light sponge.

Always fold by hand using a rubber spatula.

Test to see if the cake is cooked by lightly pressing a finger into the center of the sponge. When the cake is ready, it should spring back without leaving an impression.

PASTRY

If pastry cracks as you roll it out, or when pressing the pastry into the cake or tart pan, just press the cracks together. Scraps of pastry can be used to patch any thin or broken areas; such repairs will rarely be visible once the pastry is filled and baked.

Once a pastry dough is made, it should be wrapped in plastic wrap and refrigerated for a time (usually an hour or so); this helps the pastry to 'relax' so that it is less likely to shrink when baked. After the resting time, roll out the pastry and use it as specified in the recipe. If lining a pan with it, do not trim the pastry at this stage; instead, allow the pastry case to rest in the refrigerator again for about 30 minutes, then remove it, trim the edges of the pastry, and bake as instructed.

When making pastry cases (especially if you have hot hands), you may find it useful to use a pastry brush rather than your hands to push the pastry into the edges of the pan.

If a cooked pastry tart is damaged, paint the pastry with lightly beaten egg white and bake for a further few minutes. The egg white acts as a 'glue'. Alternatively, paint the inside of the pastry shell with tepid melted chocolate. This gives additional flavor and strength to the product.

Baking blind Baking blind is a technique whereby the pastry case is baked on its own until lightly colored, then allowed to cool before the filling is added. This pre-cooking ensures a crisper result than if the filling were baked in an uncooked pastry case.

To bake blind, put a layer of foil or parchment paper in the base of the chilled pastry case and fill it with ceramic pastry beads, dried beans or rice; this weighs the pastry down and ensures that it does not rise or bubble during cooking. Bake for 15–20 minutes, then remove the foil or paper and the weights, and return the pastry case to the oven for 5 minutes more, or as stated in the recipe. Allow to cool, then fill and bake as directed.

Note that beans and rice that have been used for baking may be reused several times for the same purpose, but should not be cooked and eaten.

chapter two

BASIC RECIPES

The following recipes form the foundation for many of the cakes and desserts in this book. The Golden, Chocolate and Genoise Sponge Cakes are usually brushed with a sugar syrup before use, then layered with cream or mousse fillings. The various pastry recipes can be used to line tart shells or as the crust for a cheesecake, or baked into discs to be sandwiched together with any of the fillings from Chapter 11.

GOLDEN SPONGE OR CHOCOLATE SPONGE

This dense Italian-style sponge, whether plain or as a chocolate version, forms the basis of such recipes as Lamingtons (page 49) and the Chocolate Dome (page 178).

MAKES
Two 8 inch round cakes
or one 10 inch round cake
or one 10½ x 15½ inch jelly roll

7 large eggs ▪
9 oz superfine sugar ▪
2 cups all-purpose flour ▪
2 teaspoons baking powder ▪
1 teaspoon natural vanilla extract ▪

Preheat the oven to 350°F. Butter the cake pan(s) and line with parchment paper. If using a jelly roll pan, extend the paper over two sides of the pan to allow for easy removal later.

Put the eggs and sugar in the heatproof bowl of an electric mixer over a saucepan of hot water, ensuring that the base of the bowl does not touch the water. Whisk the mixture with a wire whisk until it is warm (approximately body temperature). Remove from the pan of hot water and beat with an electric mixer on low to medium speed until the mixture is cooled, very thick and mousse-like, 5–8 minutes.

Sift the flour and baking powder together twice. Using a rubber spatula, fold the flour into the egg mixture in three batches until combined, adding the vanilla extract down the side of the bowl along with the first batch of flour.

Pour the mixture into the prepared pan(s). Smooth the surface. Bake until the cake springs back when pressed gently; this will take 25 minutes for two 8 inch round cakes, 30 minutes for one 10 inch cake, and 30–35 minutes for a jelly roll. Allow to cool in the pan(s) on a wire rack for 10 minutes, then turn out onto the wire rack, peel off the parchment paper and allow to cool completely.

VARIATION
CHOCOLATE SPONGE
Use 7 oz all-purpose flour, plus 1¾ oz unsweetened cocoa powder, preferably Dutch style, sifted together.

Tips
- Store the cake(s), wrapped in plastic wrap, in a cool place (but not in the refrigerator) for up to 3 days.
- The cake(s) may also be well wrapped and frozen for up to 3 months.

CHOCOLATE GENOISE SPONGE

This versatile French sponge cake is used for the Apricot Mousse Gateau (page 73)
and Bacio Semifreddo (page 156); or use it with a filling and frosting of your choice from those in Chapter 11.

MAKES
Two 8 inch round cakes
or one 10 inch round cake

5 large eggs ■
½ cup superfine sugar ■
3½ oz all-purpose flour ■
¼ cup unsweetened cocoa powder, ■
preferably Dutch style
¼ cup cornstarch ■
Pinch of baking soda ■
1¾ oz unsalted butter, melted and cooled slightly ■

Preheat the oven to 350°F. Butter the cake pan(s) and line with parchment paper.

Put the eggs and sugar in the heatproof bowl of an electric mixer over a saucepan of hot water, ensuring that the base of the bowl does not touch the water. Whisk the mixture with a wire whisk until it is warm (approximately body temperature). Remove from the pan of hot water and beat with an electric mixer on low to medium speed until the mixture is cooled, very thick and mousse-like, 5–8 minutes.

Sift the flour, cocoa, cornstarch and baking soda together.

Put the melted butter into a small bowl. Add about 2 tablespoons of the egg mixture to the melted butter and stir well.

Add the sifted dry ingredients to the egg mixture. Using a rubber spatula, fold in until combined. Lastly, add the butter mixture and fold in lightly. Pour the mixture into the prepared pan(s). Bake for 25–30 minutes for 8 inch cakes, or 35 minutes for a 10 inch cake, or until the cake springs away from the side of the pan.

Allow to cool in the pan(s) on a wire rack for 10 minutes, then turn out onto the wire rack, peel off the parchment paper and allow to cool completely.

VARIATIONS
NUT GENOISE
Add ½ cup ground nuts (such as hazelnuts, walnuts, pecans or brazil nuts) to the sifted dry ingredients.

CHOCOLATE CHIP GENOISE
Add ⅔ cup finely chopped dark chocolate to the flour mixture.

SWEET PIE PASTRY

*Use this classic, versatile pastry for tarts, cheesecakes,
fruit tarts and individual tartlets.*

TO LINE
Two 8 inch tart pans
or one 10 inch springform pan
or 30 small tartlet pans

2/3 cup unsalted butter, at room temperature ■
3/4 cup pure confectioner's sugar ■
2 large egg yolks ■
1/4 cup ground almonds or ground hazelnuts ■
2 cups all-purpose flour ■

Using an electric mixer or a food processor, cream the butter until pale and fluffy.

Add the confectioner's sugar, beating until combined, then add the egg yolks.

Continue beating, then add the ground nuts and sifted flour and beat until just combined.

Turn the dough out onto a lightly floured work surface and bring together into a ball. Wrap in plastic wrap and allow to rest in the refrigerator for 1 hour. Remove from the refrigerator and leave for about 5 minutes to return to room temperature, then roll out on a lightly floured surface, and use as directed in the recipe.

CHOCOLATE PASTRY

*This basic pie pastry can be used in the usual way,
or baked into discs to be sandwiched together with mousse or cream fillings.*

TO LINE
One 8–8½ inch tart pan
or 30 small tartlet pans

½ cup unsalted butter, chopped, ■
at room temperature
3½ oz superfine sugar ■
1 large egg yolk ■
7 oz all-purpose flour ■
1¾ oz unsweetened cocoa powder, ■
preferably Dutch style
1 teaspoon natural vanilla extract ■
2 teaspoons iced water, if needed ■

Using an electric mixer or a food processor, cream the butter and superfine sugar until pale and fluffy.

Add the egg yolk, then the sifted flour and cocoa powder, and beat until just combined.

Add the vanilla extract, and, if needed, enough iced water to bring the mixture together.

Turn the dough out onto a lightly floured work surface and bring together into a ball. Wrap in plastic wrap and allow to rest in the refrigerator for 1 hour. Remove from the refrigerator and leave for about 5 minutes to return to room temperature, then roll or press out between two sheets of parchment paper or plastic wrap to prevent it from sticking. Use as directed in the recipe.

CHOCOLATE CHIP PASTRY

*Substitute this pastry for shortcrust or other pastries when lining tart pans,
or use it as the base for a cheesecake.*

TO LINE
One 8½ inch springform pan
or two 8 inch tart pans
or 30 small tartlet pans

1¾ cups all-purpose flour ■
2 tablespoons pure confectioner's sugar ■
¼ cup lightly packed soft brown sugar ■
3½ oz unsalted butter, chopped, at room temperature ■
2 large egg yolks ■
⅓ cup grated dark chocolate ■
1 tablespoon iced water, if needed ■

Sift the flour and confectioner's sugar into a bowl, then add the brown sugar. Rub the butter into the dry ingredients until the mixture resembles breadcrumbs.

Add the egg yolks and grated chocolate and quickly work the mixture together with a knife or your hands to form a soft dough, adding a little iced water if necessary.

Turn the dough out onto a lightly floured work surface and bring together into a ball. Wrap in plastic wrap and allow to rest in the refrigerator for 1 hour. Remove from the refrigerator and leave for about 5 minutes to return to room temperature, then roll out between two sheets of parchment paper or plastic wrap and use as directed in the recipe.

CHOCOLATE CREAM PUFFS

Light as a feather, these heavenly pastries are wonderful to serve for afternoon tea. For variation, the choux pastry may be piped into finger lengths to make éclairs. Fill them with whipped cream and coat with melted dark chocolate.

MAKES 30 SMALL PUFFS OR ABOUT 18 ÉCLAIRS

CHOUX PASTRY
1 cup hot water ▪
½ cup unsalted butter ▪
1 cup all-purpose flour ▪
4 large eggs ▪
1 tablespoon unsweetened cocoa powder, ▪
preferably Dutch style

CHOCOLATE CREAM
⅔ cup chopped dark chocolate ▪
1 large egg, separated ▪
1¼ cups whipping cream ▪
2 tablespoons dark rum or liqueur (optional) ▪

Pure confectioner's sugar, for dusting ▪

Preheat the oven to 400°F. Lightly butter two baking sheets, or line them with parchment paper.

CHOUX PASTRY
Bring the water and butter to a rapid boil in a medium saucepan. Quickly add the sifted flour while stirring with a wooden spoon, and continue stirring until the mixture leaves the side of the pan.

Remove from the heat and add the eggs, one at a time, beating well after each addition. Beat in the sifted cocoa powder.

Place teaspoonfuls of the mixture on the prepared baking sheets, allowing room for spreading. Alternatively, if making éclairs, fit a piping bag with a ½ inch plain nozzle and pipe fingers of mixture about 3½–4 inches long.

Bake for 20 minutes, then reduce the oven temperature to 350°F. Bake for 15–20 minutes more, or until crisp and dry, then transfer to a wire rack and leave to cool.

CHOCOLATE CREAM
Melt the chocolate in a heatproof bowl over hot water, ensuring that the base of the bowl does not touch the water. Allow to cool slightly, then add the egg yolk. Beat until smooth.

Using an electric mixer, beat the egg white in a clean, dry bowl until stiff. Whip the cream until stiff peaks form. Using a rubber spatula, fold the beaten egg white and whipped cream into the chocolate mixture. Flavor with rum or liqueur if desired. Split open the puffs or éclairs, fill with the chocolate cream and dust with sifted confectioner's sugar.

NOTE Cream puffs or éclairs should be consumed on the day they are made.

chapter three

TRIED AND TESTED

Reliable classics and nostalgia-laden family favorites are the basis
of every cook's repertoire. These are the recipes we turn to most often, and those
that we pass on to family and friends as an act of love and generosity.

AUNT ANNIE'S HEDGEHOG

This delicious chocolate bar cookie was a highlight of my childhood holidays at my Aunt Annie's house.
It was she who introduced me to the pleasure and passion of chocolate, and I have developed this recipe in her honor.

MAKES 30

1 cup unsalted butter ■
1⅓ cups chopped dark chocolate ■
¼ cup unsweetened cocoa powder, ■
preferably Dutch style
3 large eggs ■
1 cup superfine sugar ■
Two 9 oz packages plain sweet cookies, ■
roughly crushed
1 cup roughly chopped walnuts ■
1 teaspoon natural vanilla extract ■

CHOCOLATE GLAZE
2 cups chopped dark chocolate ■
1 oz unsalted butter, chopped, at room temperature, ■
or 2 teaspoons light corn syrup

Line a 8 x 12 inch shallow cake pan with parchment paper.

Melt the butter in a saucepan. Add the chocolate and cocoa and stir until melted and combined. Do not allow to cool.

Using an electric mixer, beat the eggs and sugar for about 3 minutes, or until thick and pale. Add the hot chocolate mixture gradually to the egg mixture, beating until the mixture thickens. Set aside.

Combine the crushed cookies and walnuts. Using a rubber spatula, stir the chocolate mixture and vanilla into the cookie mixture.

Press the mixture into the prepared pan. Cover with plastic wrap and refrigerate for about 1 hour, or until firm.

CHOCOLATE GLAZE
Melt the chocolate in a heatproof bowl over hot water, ensuring that the base of the bowl does not touch the water. When melted, add the butter pieces or corn syrup, remove from the heat and stir until the butter is melted or the corn syrup incorporated. Spread the glaze over the hedgehog. Refrigerate for about 20 minutes, until the glaze is set, then slice into small rectangles.

NOTE The glaze can be made with either butter, which gives a firm, dull glaze, or corn syrup, which produces a glossy but slightly less firm glaze.

CARROT AND WALNUT CAKE

Vegetables and cake may seem unlikely partners, but they pair extremely well in this modern classic.
A lemony cream-cheese frosting provides a delicious finishing touch.

SERVES 8

10 ½ oz all-purpose flour ▪
1 teaspoon baking powder ▪
1 teaspoon baking soda ▪
½ teaspoon ground cinnamon ▪
4 large eggs ▪
9 oz superfine sugar ▪
1¼ cups grated dark chocolate ▪
½ cup chopped walnuts ▪
2 cups firmly packed coarsely grated carrot ▪
(3 small to medium carrots)
1 cup vegetable oil ▪

LEMON FROSTING
½ cup cream cheese, at room temperature ▪
½ cup unsalted butter, at room temperature ▪
2 cups confectioner's sugar, sifted ▪
2 tablespoons fresh lemon juice ▪

Toasted shredded coconut, for decoration (optional) ▪

Preheat the oven to 350°F. Butter two 8 inch round cake pans and line the bases with parchment paper.

Sift the dry ingredients together.

In a large bowl, using an electric mixer, beat the eggs and sugar until pale and increased in volume, about 5 minutes.

Add the sifted dry ingredients and fold in using a rubber spatula. Add the grated chocolate, walnuts, carrot and oil and fold in. Do not over-mix.

Pour the mixture into the pans and bake for 45–50 minutes, or until cooked when tested with a skewer. Allow to cool in the pans for 10 minutes, then turn out onto a wire rack to cool completely.

LEMON FROSTING
Beat all the ingredients together until light and fluffy. Use the frosting to fill and frost the cake. If desired, decorate with the coconut.

VARIATIONS

1 small can crushed pineapple, drained, or 1½ cups coarsely grated granny smith apple may be added to this recipe.

This cake can also be made in a 8 x 12 inch pan, baked for 45–50 minutes, then frosted and cut into squares. If cut into squares of approximately 2 inches, it will make 24 pieces.

Tip
▪ Refrigerate the cake to allow the frosting to firm before slicing.

ONE-BOWL CHOCOLATE CAKE

This is a simply delicious family chocolate cake, which is also easy for children to make.

SERVES 8

1½ cups self-rising flour ■
4 tablespoons unsweetened cocoa powder, ■
preferably Dutch style
½ cup unsalted butter, at room temperature ■
⅔ cup superfine sugar ■
3 large eggs ■
½ cup milk ■

CHOCOLATE FROSTING
3 tablespoons unsweetened cocoa powder, ■
preferably Dutch style, sifted
2 tablespoons unsalted butter, at room temperature ■
2 cups pure confectioner's sugar, sifted ■
1 teaspoon natural vanilla extract ■
3 tablespoons milk ■

Preheat the oven to 375°F. Butter two 7 inch round cake pans and line them with parchment paper.

Sift the flour and cocoa powder together into a mixing bowl. Add the butter, superfine sugar, eggs and milk. Using an electric mixer on low speed, beat the ingredients together until combined. Increase the speed and continue to beat for a further 2 minutes, or until the mixture is pale in color. Divide the mixture evenly between the prepared pans and smooth the surface. Bake for 25 minutes, or until cooked when tested with a skewer.

Allow to cool in the pans on a wire rack for 10 minutes, then turn out onto the wire rack and allow to cool completely.

CHOCOLATE FROSTING
Place the cocoa, butter, confectioner's sugar, vanilla and milk in a bowl. Using an electric mixer, beat until combined and of a spreadable consistency. Use the frosting to fill and frost the cake.

DEVIL'S FOOD CAKE

This dark, dense cake is an American classic. Use Dutch-style cocoa powder if you can; this gives the cake its deep, rich color.

SERVES 8

½ cup unsalted butter, at room temperature ■
9 oz superfine sugar ■
2 large eggs, beaten ■
1 teaspoon natural vanilla extract ■
2/3 cup unsweetened cocoa powder, ■
preferably Dutch style
½ cup hot water ■
2 teaspoons white vinegar ■
1 cup milk ■
1¾ cups all-purpose flour ■
1 teaspoon baking powder ■
1 teaspoon baking soda ■
Pinch of salt ■

CHOCOLATE VIENNA FROSTING
½ cup unsalted butter, at room temperature ■
3 tablespoons unsweetened cocoa powder, ■
preferably Dutch style
3 tablespoons hot water ■
2½ cups pure confectioner's sugar ■

Chocolate curls or rolls (page 233), to decorate ■

Preheat the oven to 350°F. Butter two 8 inch round cake pans and line them with parchment paper.

Using an electric mixer, cream the butter and sugar until pale and fluffy. Gradually add the eggs and vanilla and beat until combined.

Blend the cocoa powder with the hot water to make a smooth paste. Gradually add this to the creamed mixture.

Add the vinegar to the milk to sour it.

Sift together the flour, baking powder, baking soda, and salt. Add to the creamed mixture alternately with the soured milk. Using a rubber spatula, fold in gently until combined.

Pour into the prepared pans and bake for 30 minutes, or until the tops of the cakes spring back when lightly pressed.

Allow to cool in the pans on a wire rack for 10 minutes, then turn out onto the wire rack and allow to cool completely.

CHOCOLATE VIENNA FROSTING
Using an electric mixer, beat the butter until creamy. Blend the cocoa powder with the hot water to make a smooth paste. Add the blended cocoa and sifted confectioner's sugar to the butter and beat until light in texture and creamy. Use the mixture to fill and frost the cake, then decorate with chocolate curls or rolls.

CHOCOLATE MARBLE CAKE

Originally from Germany, this delicious, moist cake keeps well, and is ideal to serve with coffee or tea.
The quantity given makes two cakes; if not eating both straight away, wrap the second well and freeze it for later.

MAKES 2 CAKES; EACH SERVES 10

2½ cups all-purpose flour ▪
2 teaspoons baking powder ▪
Pinch of salt ▪
1½ cups unsalted butter, at room temperature ▪
15¼ oz superfine sugar ▪
7 large eggs ▪
Grated zest and juice of 1 large lemon ▪
5 tablespoons dark rum ▪
3 tablespoons milk ▪
½ teaspoon baking soda ▪
2 cups chopped dark chocolate, melted ▪

Preheat the oven to 350°F.

Butter two loaf pans 5½ x 8½ inches x 2¾ inches deep, and line them with parchment paper.

Sift the flour, baking powder and salt together.

Using an electric mixer, cream the butter and sugar until pale and fluffy. Beat in the eggs one at a time, beating well. (The mixture may appear to separate; this does not matter.)

Beat in the lemon zest, juice and 2 tablespoons of the rum. Using a rubber spatula, fold in the dry ingredients. Spoon half the mixture into a separate bowl.

Stir the remaining rum, the milk and baking soda into the melted chocolate. Beat until smooth, then beat with a rubber spatula into one half of the cake mixture.

Spoon alternating batches of the plain and chocolate mixtures into the pans. Tap the pans a couple of times to level the mixtures, then cut through the mixture with a knife from corner to corner to create the marbled effect. Bake for about 45 minutes, or until cooked when tested with a skewer.

Allow the cakes to cool in the pans on a wire rack for 10 minutes, then turn out onto the wire rack to cool completely.

CHOCOLATE CHUNK COOKIES

The use of brown sugar in these simple, crowd-pleasing cookies helps the chocolate chunks to keep their shape when baked.

MAKES 30–36

1 tablespoon instant coffee granules ■
2 tablespoons boiling water ■
7 oz all-purpose flour ■
1/4 teaspoon baking soda ■
3/4 cup unsalted butter, at room temperature ■
3/4 cup superfine sugar ■
1/2 cup firmly packed soft brown sugar ■
1 large egg ■
1 teaspoon natural vanilla extract ■
1 2/3 cups roughly chopped dark chocolate ■
1 1/2 cups chopped unsalted walnuts or pecans ■

Lightly butter two baking sheets.

Dissolve the coffee granules in the boiling water. Allow to cool.

Sift the flour and baking soda together.

Using an electric mixer, cream the butter and sugars together until pale and fluffy. Beat in the dissolved coffee, the egg and vanilla.

Add the flour and stir with a wooden spoon until the mixture is well blended. Add the chopped chocolate and nuts, mixing thoroughly.

Cover the mixture and chill for 30 minutes.

Meanwhile, preheat the oven to 325°F.

Roll about 1 tablespoon of dough at a time into a ball the size of a walnut and place on the prepared sheets, allowing room for the cookies to spread. Bake for 12–15 minutes, or until golden brown.

Allow to firm on the sheets for 5 minutes, then transfer to a wire rack to cool.

CHOCOLATE CHIP MUFFINS

The secret of light, tender muffins is not to overmix them; stir just until the ingredients are combined.
It doesn't matter if the mixture is still a little lumpy.

MAKES 12 LARGE OR 16 STANDARD

2 cups all-purpose flour ■
1 tablespoon baking powder ■
¼ cup unsweetened cocoa powder, ■
preferably Dutch style
4½ oz superfine sugar ■
1½ cups dark chocolate chips ■
2 large eggs, beaten ■
1¼ cups milk ■
⅓ cup unsalted butter, melted ■

Preheat the oven to 375°F. Butter muffin pans or line the cups with paper liners.

Sift the flour, baking powder, cocoa and sugar into a large bowl. Add half the chocolate chips.

Combine the eggs, milk and melted butter. Using a wooden spoon, gently stir into the dry ingredients, being careful not to overmix. Divide the mixture evenly among the muffin pans. Sprinkle the remaining chocolate chips over the muffins.

Bake for about 20 minutes, or until cooked when tested with a skewer. Allow to cool in the pans on a wire rack for 5 minutes, then turn out onto the wire rack and allow to cool completely.

TRIPLE CHOCOLATE MUFFINS

MAKES 12 LARGE OR 16 STANDARD

½ cup unsalted butter, at room temperature ■
½ cup superfine sugar ■
½ cup lightly packed soft brown sugar ■
2 large eggs, lightly beaten ■
1⅓ cups chopped dark chocolate, melted and cooled ■
2 cups all-purpose flour ■
1 tablespoon baking powder ■
¼ cup unsweetened cocoa powder, ■
preferably Dutch style
1 cup milk ■
⅔ cup dark chocolate, chopped into small chunks ■

Chocolate Butter Frosting (page 225) ■

Preheat the oven to 375°F. Butter muffin pans or line the cups with paper liners.

Using an electric mixer, cream the butter and sugars until pale and fluffy. Gradually beat in the eggs, then the tepid melted chocolate.

Sift the flour, baking powder and cocoa powder together and add to the mixture. Using a rubber spatula, fold the dry ingredients into the butter mixture until just combined (do not overmix), then stir in the chocolate chunks. Divide the mixture evenly among the muffin pans.

Bake for 20–25 minutes, or until firm to the touch. Allow to cool in the pans on a wire rack for 5 minutes, then turn out onto the wire rack and allow to cool completely. Coat with chocolate butter frosting. Allow to set, then store in an airtight container.

LAMINGTONS

This classic Australian recipe is enduringly popular for fund raising, country fairs and children's birthday parties. Make the base sponge the day before, so it will be firmer to cut.

MAKES 35

1 quantity Golden Sponge (page 30), ■
baked the day before in a 8 x 12 inch pan
9 oz grated dried, or shredded, coconut ■
6 cups pure confectioner's sugar ■
¾ cup unsweetened cocoa powder, ■
preferably Dutch style
2½ oz unsalted butter, chopped ■
½ teaspoon natural vanilla extract ■
7½ fl oz boiling water ■

Cut the cake into five strips lengthwise, then cut each strip into seven even pieces.

Sprinkle the coconut onto a sheet of parchment paper.

Sift the confectioner's sugar and cocoa into a heatproof bowl. Add the butter, vanilla extract and boiling water. Stir until smooth. Place the bowl over a saucepan of hot water, ensuring that the base of the bowl does not touch the water, and stir for 2–3 minutes. The frosting should be thin; add a little more boiling water if necessary.

Keeping the bowl over the hot water while working, dip each square of cake briefly into the frosting, using two forks or your hand. Allow the excess to drip back into the bowl. Roll each square in coconut to coat, then place on a wire rack to set. Repeat to coat all the squares.

Store in an airtight container at room temperature for 2–3 days.

CHOCOLATE MASCARPONE REFRIGERATOR CAKE

In the 1950s, this no-bake recipe was immensely popular for children's birthday parties. Although the cake still retains its nostalgic appeal, the addition of mascarpone cheese gives this version a more sophisticated twist.

SERVES 6–8

1½ cups whipping cream ▪
4½ oz mascarpone cheese ▪
⅔ cup chopped dark or milk chocolate, melted ▪
¾ cup chopped white chocolate, melted ▪
9 oz package plain chocolate cookies; ▪
thin ones work best. Or use Chocolate Cookies (page 57),
omitting the frosting
Chocolate curls or rolls (page 233), for decoration ▪

Line a baking sheet with parchment paper.

In the bowl of an electric mixer, whip the cream to soft peaks. Add the mascarpone cheese and continue beating just until stiff peaks form. (Be careful when beating mascarpone cheese, as it 'splits' if overbeaten).

Place half the cream mixture into another bowl.

Stir the cooled melted dark or milk chocolate into one bowl of the cream mixture and the cooled melted white chocolate into the other, to give brown and white mixtures.

Generously spread the dark chocolate cream mixture on the cookies and place them on the prepared baking sheet, upright and at an angle, to form a log shape. Refrigerate for 1–2 hours, or until firm.

Spread the white chocolate cream mixture over the log to cover the top, sides and ends. Refrigerate the log cake overnight to allow the cookies to soften and the flavors to meld.

To serve, place the chilled cake on a serving plate and decorate with chocolate curls. Cut into slices and serve immediately.

VARIATION
If you are intending to serve this cake to adults rather than children, 1–2 tablespoons of the liqueur of your choice can be added to the filling mixture.

CHOCOLATE CONTINENTAL ROLL

The fillings for this simple but elegant cake can be varied. Try spreading it with a layer of melted chocolate or ganache, then with whipped cream as below; or fill the cake with fresh raspberries and chocolate mousse instead of cream.

SERVES 8

4½ oz chopped dark chocolate ▪
3 tablespoons freshly brewed strong black coffee ▪
4 large eggs, separated ▪
6½ oz superfine sugar ▪
1 teaspoon unsweetened cocoa powder, ▪
preferably Dutch style
7 fl oz whipping cream, whipped to stiff peaks ▪

Preheat the oven to 350°F. Butter a 10 x 12 inch cake pan and line with parchment paper.

Add the chocolate to the coffee and allow to melt, then leave until cool, stirring occasionally.

Using an electric mixer, beat the egg yolks and sugar until pale and creamy and the beaters leave a ribbon-like trail when lifted from the mixture. Add the chocolate mixture and mix well.

Using an electric mixer and clean, dry beaters, beat the egg whites in a clean, dry bowl until stiff peaks form, then gently fold into the chocolate mixture.

Pour into the prepared pan and bake for 12 minutes. Turn off the heat and leave the cake in the oven, with the door closed, for a further 10 minutes.

Remove from the oven and lightly dust the surface with sifted cocoa powder. Cover with a clean, damp cloth and allow to cool.

Turn out carefully onto a sheet of parchment paper. Remove the paper from the bottom of the cake. Spread with the whipped cream and roll up from one of the long sides, using the paper to assist you. Cut into slices to serve.

CHOCOLATE SELF-SAUCING PUDDING

As well as being delicious, self-saucing puddings are like culinary sleight of hand; the sauce starts out on the top but ends up at the bottom.

SERVES 6

½ cup unsalted butter, chopped ■
⅔ cup chopped dark chocolate ■
2 large eggs ■
3¼ oz superfine sugar ■
1 teaspoon natural vanilla extract ■
1 cup self-rising flour ■
2 tablespoons unsweetened cocoa powder, ■
preferably Dutch style
½ cup milk ■

SAUCE
½ cup firmly packed soft brown sugar ■
2 tablespoons unsweetened cocoa powder, ■
preferably Dutch style
1 cup boiling water ■

Pure confectioner's sugar, for dusting ■

Preheat the oven to 350°F. Butter a 6 cup ovenproof dish.

Melt the butter and chocolate in a saucepan. Allow to cool.

Lightly beat the eggs, superfine sugar and vanilla extract together. Add to the cooled chocolate mixture.

Sift the flour and cocoa powder together, then, using a rubber spatula, fold into the chocolate mixture alternately with the milk. Pour the batter into the prepared dish.

SAUCE
Mix the brown sugar and sifted cocoa powder together and sprinkle over the mixture. Pour the boiling water gently over the surface and bake for 40–45 minutes, or until the top has formed a crust and a skewer inserted halfway into the cake comes out clean.

Dust with confectioner's sugar and serve warm or hot with ice cream or lightly whipped cream.

VARIATIONS
After you have added the flour and milk, add any of the following variations:

⅓ cup toasted, peeled and chopped hazelnuts; plus ¼ cup chocolate chips; plus 3 tablespoons raisins, cut in half and soaked in 2½ tablespoons brandy for 2 hours or overnight. Add both the raisins and the brandy to the mixture.

⅓ cup chopped dates

⅓ cup cherries, pitted, halved and soaked in orange liqueur, such as Cointreau

CHOCOLATE PAVLOVA

This cream-and-fruit-topped meringue cake, crisp on the outside and marshmallowy in the center, was created in Australia to honor the ballerina Anna Pavlova. Quantities are given for both a medium and large version.

8 INCH; SERVES 8

A little sifted combined cornstarch ■
and pure confectioner's sugar, for dusting
4 large egg whites, at room temperature ■
Pinch of salt ■
1 cup white sugar ■
¼ cup superfine sugar ■
2 teaspoons cornstarch ■
1 tablespoon unsweetened cocoa powder, ■
preferably Dutch style
1 teaspoon white vinegar ■
Few drops natural vanilla extract ■

FILLING
1¼ cups whipping cream ■
Pure confectioner's sugar, sifted, to taste ■
Few drops natural vanilla extract or liqueur, such as Kirsch ■
10½ oz fruit of your choice (such as hulled and ■
cleaned berries, stone fruit, kiwifruit, passionfruit pulp)

10 INCH; SERVES 12

A little sifted combined cornstarch ■
and pure confectioner's sugar, for dusting
8 large egg whites, at room temperature ■
Pinch of salt ■
2 cups white sugar ■
½ cup superfine sugar ■
1 tablespoon cornstarch ■
2 tablespoons unsweetened cocoa powder, ■
preferably Dutch style
1 teaspoon white vinegar ■
1 teaspoon natural vanilla extract ■

FILLING
2 cups whipping cream ■
Pure confectioner's sugar, sifted, to taste ■
1 teaspoon natural vanilla extract or liqueur, such as Kirsch ■
1 lb fruit of your choice (such as hulled and ■
cleaned berries, stone fruit, kiwifruit, passionfruit pulp)

Preheat the oven to 300°F. Draw a 8 inch or 10 inch circle on parchment paper or foil placed on a baking sheet. Butter the circle, then sprinkle with the sifted combined cornstarch and confectioner's sugar.

In a large, clean, dry bowl, using an electric mixer, beat the egg whites and salt first on medium speed, then on high speed until stiff peaks form.

Add the combined white and caster sugars, 1 tablespoon at a time, beating well after each addition to dissolve the sugar. With the last amount of sugar, add the cornstarch and sifted cocoa powder, then, using a rubber spatula, fold in the vinegar and vanilla extract.

Spread the chocolate meringue to cover the circle and shape it into a cake, dome or pie-shell shape, as preferred.

Bake for 15 minutes, then reduce the oven temperature to 235°F and bake for a further 1¼ hours for a 8 inch pavlova, or 1½ hours for a 10 inch pavlova, or until crisp and dry. Allow to cool in the oven.

Remove from the oven. Peel away the paper or foil and place on a serving plate.

To make the filling, whip the cream to stiff peaks, then sweeten it with sifted confectioner's sugar and vanilla extract or liqueur. Spread the pavlova with the whipped cream and top with the fruit.

VARIATION
CHOCOLATE COFFEE CREAM
Whip the cream, then flavor it with a little sifted cocoa powder, coffee liqueur and confectioner's sugar to taste. Decorate with chocolate curls or rolls (page 233).

FUDGY BROWNIES

Ready in less than an hour, these fudgy treats are delightfully sweet and rich.

MAKES 15

½ cup unsalted butter ▪
⅔ cup chopped dark chocolate ▪
1 cup superfine sugar ▪
2 large eggs ▪
1 teaspoon natural vanilla extract ▪
¾ cup all-purpose flour ▪
¾ cup chopped walnuts ▪

½ quantity Chocolate Ganache Glaze (page 229; optional) ▪

Preheat the oven to 350°F. Butter a shallow 7 inch square cake pan and line it with parchment paper, extending the paper up over two sides of the pan to allow for easy removal later.

Melt the butter in a medium saucepan over low heat. Add the chopped chocolate, stir until smooth, then allow to cool.

Using an electric mixer, beat the sugar and eggs together and then stir into the cooled chocolate mixture along with the vanilla extract. Using a rubber spatula, fold in the sifted flour, then stir in the chopped walnuts.

Pour the mixture into the prepared pan and bake for 30–35 minutes. Check the mixture 2–3 minutes before the end of the suggested baking time; the top should be firm. To ensure a fudgy texture, brownies are better undercooked than overcooked. Allow to cool in the pan.

If frosting with the Chocolate Ganache Glaze, chill it to a spreadable consistency, then spread over the top of the brownies. Cut into squares and store in an airtight container.

CHOCOLATE COOKIES

Crisp, plain chocolate cookies are great for children's lunchboxes or to have on hand for afternoon tea or a snack.
They can also be used, minus the frosting, as the basis for the Chocolate Mascarpone Refrigerator Cake on page 50.

MAKES 36

½ cup unsalted butter, chopped ▪
1 cup chopped dark chocolate ▪
1 cup lightly packed soft brown sugar ▪
1 large egg ▪
1 teaspoon natural vanilla extract ▪
1⅔ cups self-rising flour ▪

FROSTING
1 cup chopped dark chocolate ▪
¼ cup unsalted butter ▪

Preheat the oven to 350°F. Line two baking sheets with parchment paper.

Melt the butter in a saucepan. Add the chocolate, remove from the heat and stir until smooth.

Combine the sugar, egg and vanilla extract in a bowl and stir well. Stir this mixture into the chocolate mixture.

Sift the flour over the chocolate mixture and, using a rubber spatula, fold in until combined. Cover and refrigerate the dough for about 20 minutes to allow it to firm a little.

Roll heaped teaspoonfuls of the mixture into balls and place on the prepared sheets, allowing room for them to spread. Bake two sheets at a time for 12–15 minutes. Allow to cool on the sheets for about 5 minutes, then transfer to a wire rack. The surface of the cookies will crack a little as they cook, and more as they cool.

FROSTING
To make the frosting, melt the chocolate and butter together over low heat and stir until smooth. Allow the frosting to cool and thicken a little before spreading. Spoon a little frosting on each cookie and spread to within about ½ inch of the edge of the cookie. Allow to set, then store in an airtight container.

TRADITIONAL SWISS CHOCOLATE MOUSSE

Rich and luscious, mousse is among the simplest of chocolate desserts to prepare, but it never fails to impress, especially when served in pretty glasses or delicate little bowls or teacups.

SERVES 4

1 cup chopped dark chocolate ▪
4 large eggs, separated ▪
1 tablespoon superfine sugar ▪

Chocolate curls or rolls (page 233), to decorate ▪

Melt the chocolate in a heatproof bowl over a saucepan of hot water, ensuring that the base of the bowl does not touch the water. Remove the bowl from the heat.

Beat the egg yolks and gradually stir into the hot melted chocolate.

Using an electric mixer and clean beaters, beat the egg whites in a clean, dry bowl until soft peaks form. Sprinkle the sugar over the egg whites and continue beating until the sugar is dissolved and the meringue is glossy. Do not overbeat.

Using a rubber spatula, fold the meringue into the warm chocolate mixture and continue gently folding until thoroughly mixed. Divide the mixture among four 7 fl oz ramekins, small bowls or glasses and chill for 4 hours or overnight.

Before serving, remove the mousse from the refrigerator and allow it to come to room temperature.

VARIATIONS
For true chocoholics, the chocolate content may be increased to 1⅓ cups.

1 tablespoon brandy, dark rum or orange liqueur may be added to the recipe at the end, when folding through the meringue.

SOUR CREAM CAKE

The smooth texture and slightly acid richness of sour cream meld beautifully with chocolate in this dense cake. It can be served as is, or used as the foundation of the Black Forest Cherry Cake (page 79).

SERVES 8–10

4½ oz chopped dark chocolate ▪
1 cup boiling water ▪
1 teaspoon baking soda ▪
1 cup unsalted butter, at room temperature ▪
11½ oz superfine sugar ▪
3 large eggs, separated ▪
1 teaspoon natural vanilla extract ▪
2½ cups all-purpose flour ▪
1 teaspoon baking powder ▪
⅔ cup sour cream (see Tip) ▪

DECORATION
14 fl oz whipping cream ▪
½ cup flaked almonds, toasted ▪
Chocolate curls or rolls (page 233) ▪

Preheat the oven to 350°F. Butter two 8 inch round cake pans and line the bases with parchment paper.

Put the chocolate in a small heatproof bowl and pour the boiling water over the top. Stir in the baking soda and allow to cool until tepid.

Using an electric mixer, cream the butter and sugar until pale and fluffy. Gradually add the egg yolks, then the vanilla extract, then the cooled chocolate mixture. (Note that the mixture may appear to separate; this does not matter.)

Sift the flour and baking powder together. Add to the mixture in two batches, alternately with the sour cream, and fold in using a rubber spatula.

Using clean beaters, beat the egg whites until stiff but not dry and fold gently into the chocolate mixture.

Divide the mixture evenly between the prepared pans and bake for 40–45 minutes, or until cooked when tested with a skewer. Allow to cool in the pans on a wire rack for 10 minutes, then turn out onto the wire rack to cool completely.

To decorate, whip the cream until stiff peaks form. Spread half of the cream over the bottom of one cake, place the other cake on top, right side up, and spread the remaining cream on top. Sprinkle with almonds and chocolate curls or rolls.

Tip
▪ Instead of sour cream, you can use whipping cream soured with 2 teaspoons lemon juice.

CHOCOLATE POUND CAKE

*Plain but delicious, pound cake is a classic butter cake that keeps well.
It is ideal for children's lunchboxes or as the basis for a chocolate trifle.*

SERVES 16

1 cup unsalted butter, at room temperature ■
9 oz superfine sugar ■
4 large eggs, beaten ■
1 tablespoon natural vanilla extract ■
2 cups all-purpose flour ■
2 teaspoons baking powder ■
½ teaspoon baking soda ■
½ cup unsweetened cocoa powder, ■
preferably Dutch style
¼ cup milk ■

Glossy Chocolate Frosting (page 225) ■

Preheat the oven to 360°F. Butter a 8 inch square cake pan and line the base with parchment paper.

Using an electric mixer, cream the butter and sugar until pale and fluffy. Gradually add the egg and vanilla and beat until combined.

Sift the flour, baking powder, baking soda and cocoa together. Add half the sifted dry ingredients to the creamed mixture and fold through using a rubber spatula. Add half the milk and stir through. Repeat with the remaining dry ingredients and milk. Beat the mixture until the ingredients are combined and smooth.

Pour the batter into the prepared pan and smooth the surface with a spatula. Bake for 45–50 minutes, or until a skewer inserted in the center comes out clean.

Allow the cake to cool in the pan on a wire rack for 10 minutes, then turn out onto the wire rack to cool completely.

When cold, frost with Glossy Chocolate Frosting.

CHOCOLATE ROUGH BAR COOKIE

My memories of this bar cookie are nostalgic of the 1960s, of teaching and The Beatles.

MAKES 16

PASTRY BASE
½ cup unsalted butter, at room temperature ■
¼ cup superfine sugar ■
1 teaspoon natural vanilla extract ■
1 cup self-rising flour ■
½ cup grated dried coconut ■

CHOCOLATE TOPPING
⅔ cup chopped dark chocolate, melted ■
½ cup sweetened condensed milk ■
1 teaspoon natural vanilla extract ■
1 cup pure confectioner's sugar, sifted ■
1 oz unsalted butter, melted ■
1 cup grated dried coconut ■

Preheat the oven to 350°F. Butter a 8 x 12 inch shallow cake pan and line it with parchment paper, extending the paper over two sides of the pan to allow for easy removal later.

PASTRY BASE
Using an electric mixer, cream the butter, sugar and vanilla until pale and fluffy. Add the sifted flour and the coconut and, using a rubber spatula, fold in thoroughly. Using slightly dampened fingers, press the mixture into the prepared pan (it will be quite soft and sticky). Bake for 25 minutes, until pale golden in color.

CHOCOLATE TOPPING
Meanwhile, combine all the topping ingredients in a bowl and mix thoroughly. As soon as the pastry is removed from the oven, spread the chocolate topping over it. Allow to cool in the pan on a wire rack, then remove from the pan, cut into squares and store in an airtight container.

DOUBLE CHOCOLATE YO-YOS

These melt-in-the-mouth chocolate shortbreads are sandwiched together with chocolate buttercream.
The recipe makes plenty; just as well, as they are sure to be popular.

MAKES 36 DOUBLE COOKIES

1 cup unsalted butter, chopped, ■
at room temperature
½ cup pure confectioner's sugar, sifted ■
4½ oz dark chocolate, melted and cooled to tepid ■
3 cups all-purpose flour ■
½ cup custard powder or cornstarch ■
1 teaspoon natural vanilla extract ■

CHOCOLATE BUTTER FROSTING
⅓ cup unsalted butter, at room temperature ■
1 cup pure confectioner's sugar, sifted ■
¼ cup dark chocolate, melted and cooled to tepid ■
1 teaspoon natural vanilla extract ■

Preheat the oven to 325°F. Lightly butter two baking sheets, or line them with parchment paper.

Using an electric mixer, cream the butter and confectioner's sugar until pale and fluffy, then add the tepid melted chocolate.

Sift the flour and custard powder or cornstarch and add to the creamed mixture. Work the mixture using a rubber spatula to form a stiff dough, adding the vanilla extract halfway through.

Roll teaspoonfuls of mixture into balls and place on the prepared sheets, allowing room for them to spread. Use the back of a fork dipped in flour to flatten each ball.

Bake for 20–25 minutes, depending on the size of the cookies. To check if they are cooked, use a spatula to lift a cookie off the sheet; if it is evenly colored underneath, with no uncooked dough visible in the center, then it is cooked. Allow the cookies to cool on the sheet for 5 minutes before transferring to a wire rack to cool completely.

CHOCOLATE BUTTER FROSTING
Using an electric mixer, cream the butter until pale and fluffy, then add the confectioner's sugar gradually. Add the cooled melted chocolate and vanilla extract and beat until thoroughly combined.

Join the cookies together in pairs with the chocolate buttercream. Allow to set, then store in an airtight container.

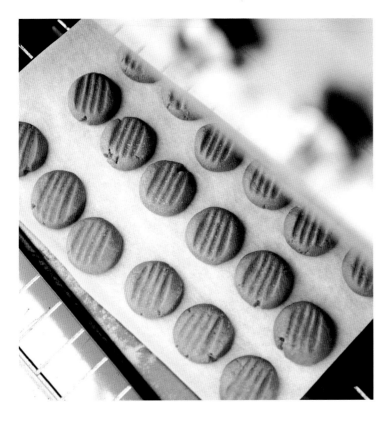

CHOCOLATE CHIFFON CAKE

This cake's name reflects its delicate and airy texture, which is best achieved by baking it in an angel food cake pan. A deep ring pan can also be used.

SERVES 8–10

3/4 cup all-purpose flour ▪
1 3/4 oz unsweetened cocoa powder, ▪
preferably Dutch style
1 1/2 teaspoons baking powder ▪
7 1/2 oz superfine sugar ▪
5 large eggs, separated ▪
1/3 cup vegetable oil ▪
Juice of 1/2 lemon ▪
Easy Chocolate Glaze (page 226); ▪
you will need a half-quantity to frost the top of the cake only,
or 1 quantity to frost both the top and the sides

Preheat the oven to 350°F. Butter a 10 inch angel food cake pan or deep ring pan. Line the base with parchment paper.

Sift the flour, cocoa and baking powder together into a large bowl. Add 1/4 cup of the sugar, the egg yolks, oil and lemon juice. Whisk by hand using a strong wire whisk until combined. The mixture will be very heavy.

Using an electric mixer, beat the egg whites in a clean, dry bowl until stiff peaks form. Continue beating on high speed while adding the remaining sugar, a tablespoon at a time, to form a thick meringue; this should take about 3 minutes. The meringue should be glossy but not dry.

Using a rubber spatula, fold half the meringue into the chocolate mixture. Return the chocolate mixture to the remaining meringue and fold until combined. Blend well; the mixture will be quite lumpy.

Pour the mixture into the prepared pan. Bake for 20–25 minutes, or until a skewer inserted into the center of the cake comes out clean. Allow to cool in the pan on a wire rack for 10 minutes, then turn out onto the wire rack to cool completely. If using an angel food pan, invert the pan and allow the cake to suspend upside down over a rack, which will cause it to drop and create a light texture.

When cool, glaze with the Chocolate Glaze.

chapter four

FRUIT AND CHOCOLATE

Due to their similar combination of acidity and sweetness,
chocolate and fruit are deliciously compatible ingredients. Seasonal fruits can be
the signature of a chocolate cake, adding texture, distinctive flavor, and a gloriously
vivid color palette. Chocolate and stone fruits, chocolate and citrus, chocolate
and berries—all are wonderful combinations to stir the senses.

APPLE AND RUM CHOCOLATE CAKE

Prepare the cake batter before making the apple and rum mixture.

SERVES 10

Preheat the oven to 350°F. Butter a 10 inch ring pan and line the base with parchment paper.

CAKE

7 oz unsalted butter, at room temperature ▪
1 cup lightly packed soft brown sugar ▪
3 large eggs, lightly beaten ▪
1 cup chopped dark chocolate, melted and cooled ▪
2¼ cups self-rising flour ▪
2 tablespoons milk ▪

CAKE

Using an electric mixer, cream the butter and sugar until pale and fluffy. Add the eggs gradually, beating continuously, then stir in the cooled melted chocolate.

Sift the flour and, using a rubber spatula, fold it into the creamed mixture. Stir in the milk.

APPLE AND RUM MIXTURE

2 golden delicious or granny smith apples ▪
½ cup golden raisins or raisins ▪
1 tablespoon dark rum ▪
1 teaspoon ground ginger ▪
½ teaspoon ground cinnamon ▪

Pure confectioner's sugar, for dusting ▪
Whipped cream, to serve ▪

APPLE AND RUM MIXTURE

Peel, core and thinly slice the apples. Combine in a bowl with the golden raisins, rum, ginger and cinnamon. Stir to coat the apples.

Divide the cake mixture in half. Spread one half in the base of the prepared pan. Spread the apple slices over the cake mixture in the pan. Gently spoon the remaining cake mixture on top of the apple layer, then smooth the surface with a spatula.

Bake for 40–45 minutes, or until cooked when tested with a skewer. If the cake is browning too much toward the end of the baking time, cover it with foil. Allow to cool in the pan on a wire rack for 10 minutes, then turn out onto the wire rack and allow to cool completely.

Dust with sifted confectioner's sugar, and serve the cake with whipped cream.

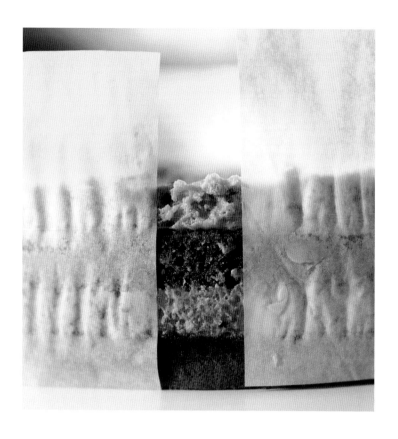

APRICOT MOUSSE CAKE

This spectacular cake for a special occasion combines a delicate and fragrant mousse, dense bands of chocolate cake, and contrasting apricot layers.

SERVES 12

One quantity Chocolate Genoise Sponge Cake(page 31), ▪
baked in a 10 inch round pan
½ cup sugar syrup (page 219) flavored with ▪
2 tablespoons orange liqueur, such as Grand Marnier

APRICOT MOUSSE
1⅔ cups dried apricots ▪
¼ cup honey (select a delicately flavored honey) ▪
¼ cup sugar ▪
2 large egg whites ▪
2 teaspoons powdered gelatin ▪
1 cup whipping cream ▪

DECORATION
10–12 fresh apricots, poached and sliced, ▪
if in season; or dried apricots, poached in sugar syrup
(page 219) for about 3 minutes or until tender,
then drained and sliced (optional)
Chocolate leaves (page 233; optional) ▪

APRICOT MOUSSE
Put the apricots and ½ cup water in a saucepan and bring to a boil. Simmer until the apricots are tender and the water evaporates. Allow to cool slightly, then blend the apricots to a purée.

Put the honey, sugar and 1½ fl oz water in a small saucepan, bring to a boil and boil for 2 minutes.

Using an electric mixer, beat the egg whites in a clean, dry bowl until soft peaks form. While beating on medium speed, gently pour in the hot syrup (avoid pouring it on the beaters, as it will spatter) and beat until cold, 5–8 minutes.

Combine the gelatin and 2 tablespoons water in a small heatproof bowl, stir to soften the gelatin, then place over a bowl of hot water, and stir until the gelatin is dissolved. Stir thoroughly into the apricot purée. Using a rubber spatula, fold in the meringue.

Whip the cream until stiff peaks form, then fold it into the apricot mousse mixture.

ASSEMBLY
Slice the Genoise Sponge horizontally into two rounds. Place one round onto a cake board, if you have one, or onto the platter on which the cake will be served, or on a round of cardboard covered with foil. Place a 10–10½ inch cake ring around the cake; if you don't have a cake ring, secure a deep collar of parchment paper around the cake. Brush the cake with the sugar syrup. Arrange the apricot slices, if using, over the sponge. Cover with half the apricot mousse. Place the second sponge layer on top and brush with sugar syrup. Cover with the remaining mousse and smooth the surface. Refrigerate for at least 3 hours, or overnight.

To serve, run a small sharp knife between the edge of the cake and the cake ring or parchment paper to loosen, then carefully remove it. Decorate with fresh apricots, if in season, or slivers of dried apricot, and chocolate leaves.

VARIATION
Dried cherries may replace the dried apricots; decorate with pitted fresh cherries.

COCOA BANANA CAKE

The recipe for this excellent and easy cake comes from my friend Jennifer Migliorelli.

SERVES 12

all-purpose flour and unsweetened cocoa powder, for dusting ▪

1½ cups mashed, very ripe bananas ▪
(about 4 large bananas)
1 cup sour cream ▪
1¾ cups all-purpose flour ▪
⅔ cup unsweetened cocoa powder, ▪
preferably Dutch style
1½ teaspoons baking soda ▪
½ teaspoon salt ▪
7 oz unsalted butter, at room temperature ▪
1⅔ cups superfine sugar ▪
3 large eggs ▪

Easy Chocolate Glaze (page 226; optional) ▪
Pure confectioner's sugar, for dusting ▪

Preheat the oven to 350°F. Butter and flour a 10 cup (88 fl oz) gugelhopf mold and dust with the sifted combined flour and cocoa powder.

Mix together the bananas and sour cream. Set aside.

Sift together the flour, cocoa, baking soda and salt.

Using an electric mixer, beat the butter and sugar until pale and fluffy, then beat in the eggs, one at a time, beating until smooth after each addition.

Beat in half the flour mixture. Beat in the banana mixture, then beat in the remaining flour mixture.

Pour the batter into the prepared mold and smooth the surface. Bake for 55–60 minutes, until well risen and a skewer inserted into the center of the cake comes out clean.

Allow to cool in the mold on a wire rack for 10 minutes, then turn out onto the wire rack to cool completely. Frost with Easy Chocolate Glaze if desired, or dust with confectioner's sugar before serving.

ORANGE AND ALMOND CHOCOLATE CAKE

Orange and chocolate are wonderfully complementary flavors. Ground almonds give a dense texture and delicate nuttiness to this flourless cake, which should be made the day before it is to be served.

SERVES 8–10

CAKE
2 large oranges ■
6 large eggs ■
¼ cup unsweetened cocoa powder, ■
preferably Dutch style, plus extra for dusting
1 teaspoon baking powder ■
1⅓ cups chopped dark chocolate, melted and cooled ■
1⅓ cups superfine sugar ■
3 cups ground almonds ■

DECORATION
1 orange, unpeeled, sliced into thin rings ■
½ cup smooth apricot jam ■
1 tablespoon orange liqueur ■
Pure confectioner's sugar, for dusting (optional) ■

Preheat the oven to 350°F. Butter a 9 inch springform pan and line the base with parchment paper.

CAKE
Wash the oranges and put them whole in a small saucepan with 1 cup water. Cover with a lid, bring to a boil, then reduce the heat and simmer the oranges until tender when pierced with a skewer, about 1 hour. Remove from the heat, drain and allow to cool. Chop the oranges roughly and remove the seeds. Purée the oranges with the peel still on, in a food processor or blender.

Using an electric mixer, beat the eggs in a large bowl until pale and thick, and ribbons form when the beaters are lifted out of the mixture. Sift the cocoa powder and baking powder together. Using a rubber spatula, fold the melted chocolate, cocoa powder, baking powder and sugar into the eggs. Stir in the orange purée and the ground almonds.

Pour the mixture into the prepared pan. Bake for about 1 hour, or until cooked when tested with a skewer. (Note that this is a moist cake, so a few tiny crumbs may still cling to the skewer.) If the cake is browning too much, cover loosely with foil during the latter stages of cooking. Allow to cool in the pan on a wire rack.

DECORATION
Microwave the orange rings for 2 minutes on medium.

Combine the apricot jam and liqueur in a small saucepan and heat gently. Sieve, then glaze the top of the cake with this mixture. Position the orange rings around the side of the cake and brush with more of the jam mixture.

Alternatively, dust with sifted confectioner's sugar.

CHOCOLATE RASPBERRY CHARLOTTE

*This classic dessert is topped with a cloud of raspberry custard
that contrasts beautifully with the rich dark chocolate layer.*

SERVES 8

One 9 oz package thin lady finger cookies ▪

BAVAROIS
21 fl oz milk ▪
2 large eggs, plus 2 egg yolks ▪
4½ oz sugar ▪
5 teaspoons powdered gelatin ▪
⅓ cup hot water ▪
14 fl oz whipping cream ▪
1 cup chopped dark chocolate, melted and cooled ▪
1 tablespoon sugar, extra ▪
1 tablespoon orange-flavored liqueur, ▪
such as Cointreau, or brandy
2 cups fresh raspberries ▪

Lightly whipped cream, to serve ▪

Line the base of a 9 inch springform pan with a foil cake board, if you have one; otherwise, cover the loosened base of the pan with parchment paper or foil before fastening it into the pan. Line the side of the pan with a band of parchment paper or foil.

Trim the lady fingers so that each is square at one end. Line the inside of the pan with the cookies, placing the cut ends downwards.

BAVAROIS
Heat the milk in a saucepan, without allowing it to boil.

Using a wire whisk, whisk the eggs, egg yolks and sugar in a bowl. Gradually pour the hot milk over the egg mixture, whisking continuously until combined. Return the mixture to the saucepan and heat gently, stirring with a wooden spoon, until the mixture coats the back of the spoon. Do not allow it to boil.

Whisk the gelatin in the hot water until dissolved. Stir into the custard mixture. Strain into a bowl and allow to cool, then divide the custard mixture in half.

Whip the cream until soft peaks form.

To make the chocolate layer, fold the cooled melted chocolate into half of the custard, then fold in half of the whipped cream. Pour the mixture into the sponge-lined pan. Refrigerate until firm, about 1 hour.

Meanwhile, prepare the raspberry layer: put the extra sugar and liqueur in a small saucepan and heat gently until the sugar is dissolved. Toss the raspberries through and set aside to cool, then blend or mash it to make a purée. Pass the purée through a sieve.

Fold the sieved purée into the remaining custard, then fold in the remaining whipped cream. Chill for 1–2 hours, until thickened, then spoon it over the chocolate layer. Cover the charlotte and chill overnight. Remove carefully from the pan and peel away the parchment or foil. Serve with lightly whipped cream.

VARIATION
A variety of berry fruits can replace the raspberries.

BLACK FOREST CHERRY CAKE

Heady with liqueur, cherries and rich, rich chocolate, this is a simply fantastic cake. Bake the Chocolate Sponge the day before, or use the Sour Cream Cake (page 61) as the basis for this recipe.

SERVES 8–12

1 quantity Chocolate Sponge (page 30), baked the day before ▪
in two 8 inch round or springform pans, or one 10 inch pan

CHERRY FILLING
3½ oz superfine sugar ▪
one 1 lb 9 oz jar pitted morello cherries, strained, ▪
liquid reserved
2 tablespoons cornstarch ▪
½ teaspoon ground cinnamon ▪

SYRUP
2 tablespoons reserved cherry liquid ▪
⅓ cup liqueur, such as Kirsch or brandy ▪

LIQUEUR CREAM
2 cups whipping cream ▪
2 tablespoons pure confectioner's sugar ▪
1 tablespoon liqueur, such as Kirsch or brandy ▪

Chocolate curls or rolls (page 233), and fresh cherries, ▪
if in season, to decorate

CHERRY FILLING
Put the sugar and ¾ cup of the reserved cherry liquid in a small saucepan and heat gently.

Blend the cornstarch and cinnamon with a little extra reserved cherry liquid and add to the saucepan. Stir until the mixture boils and thickens. Add the drained cherries and refrigerate until cold.

SYRUP
Combine the reserved cherry liquid and the liqueur.

LIQUEUR CREAM
Whip the cream until stiff peaks form, then fold in the sifted confectioner's sugar and liqueur.

ASSEMBLY
If using a 10 inch cake, slice it in half horizontally. Spoon half the syrup over each cake or cake layer. Put one cake or layer on a serving plate, syrup side up, then spread the cooled cherry filling over the cake, keeping the cherries away from the edge. Spread one-third of the cream over the cherry filling. Place the second cake or layer on top, syrup side up, and spread the top and side of the cake with the remaining cream.

Decorate with chocolate curls or rolls, and cherries, if in season.

VARIATION
A classic White Forest Cake can be made using a Golden Sponge (page 30), sprinkled with liqueur such as Kirsch, spread with a good-quality raspberry or sour cherry jam, and layered with cherry filling, and freshly whipped cream.

PEAR AND FIG STRUDEL

This is an easy winter dessert—serve it hot, dusted with confectioner's sugar.
Apricots make a nice addition to this combination of flavors.

SERVES 8–10

14 oz block frozen puff pastry, thawed (see Tips) ▪
2 tablespoons butter, melted ▪
1¼ cups ginger cookies, such as ▪
gingersnaps, roughly chopped in a food processor
2 ripe pears, peeled and thinly sliced ▪
¾ cup dried figs, stalks removed, sliced ▪
½ cup chopped pistachio nuts or walnuts ▪
1 cup roughly chopped dark chocolate ▪
Extra melted butter, for glazing ▪
Pure confectioner's sugar, for dusting ▪

Whipped cream, to serve ▪

Preheat the oven to 425°F. Butter a baking sheet.

To prepare the pastry, roll it out on a lightly floured surface to measure 12 x 16 inches, working with the longest edge of the pastry towards you. Transfer the pastry to a clean dish towel or piece of parchment paper; this will assist in rolling it up.

Brush the pastry with the melted butter and sprinkle it with the crushed ginger cookies.

To make the filling, combine the pears, figs, nuts and chocolate in a bowl and stir to mix. Spread the fruit filling over the front half of the pastry only, leaving a narrow border at the short ends.

Lift the long side of the strudel closest to you and gently roll up. Brush the edges of the pastry with melted butter, then fold the ends in. Place the strudel, with the join underneath, on the prepared sheet. Brush generously with extra melted butter.

Bake for 10 minutes, then reduce the oven temperature to 350°F and bake for a further 25–30 minutes, or until golden brown.

To serve, dust with confectioner's sugar. Serve the strudel hot or cold with cream.

VARIATION
Fresh dark sour cherries, pitted, may replace the pear and figs.

Tips
▪ If blocks of puff pastry are unavailable, use two sheets of ready-rolled puff pastry, joining them end to end to give the necessary size.
▪ Filo pastry can replace the puff pastry, but allow extra melted butter for glazing the filo sheets. Use six sheets, buttering each sheet before stacking another on top.

SEVILLE MOUSSE CAKE

Any type of orange can be used for this cake, although the color of blood oranges gives a particularly pretty contrast with the layers of light mousse and dark chocolate cake.

SERVES 16

1 quantity Golden Sponge or Chocolate Sponge (page 30), ▪
baked in a 10 inch pan
6 blood oranges or other oranges ▪

MOUSSE
1¼ cups whipping cream ▪
4 egg yolks ▪
½ cup superfine sugar ▪
1 cup chopped dark, milk or white chocolate, melted ▪
2 cups whipping cream, extra ▪

FILLING AND DECORATION
1 quantity Sugar Syrup (page 219), ▪
flavored with 1 tablespoon orange liqueur
½ cup chopped toasted pistachio nuts ▪
Julienne of Candied Orange Peel (page 172) ▪

MOUSSE

Remove the zest from four of the oranges and slice it. Put the cream and zest in a saucepan and bring just to a boil, then set aside to infuse for 2 hours, or overnight.

Bring the infused cream back just to a boiling point. Meanwhile, put the egg yolks and sugar in a heatproof bowl and mix lightly to combine. Slowly pour the boiled cream through a strainer onto the yolks while stirring. Discard the zest. Pour the mixture back into the same saucepan and cook over low heat until the mixture coats the back of a wooden spoon. Do not allow it to boil.

Transfer to a large bowl. Add the melted chocolate and stir until combined. Set aside to cool. When the chocolate custard is cool, whip the extra cream to soft peaks, then fold it into the chocolate custard. Chill the mousse for 1 hour before use.

FILLING AND DECORATION

To assemble the cake, segment all six of the oranges. Slice the sponge into three pieces horizontally. Put the first layer of sponge on a cake board or serving platter and brush with some of the sugar syrup. Arrange half of the orange segments on the cake. Position a strip of parchment paper around the cake, tying it gently with string (or use a ring pan if you have one) to hold the successive layers in place as you assemble them.

Cover the sponge and orange segments with one-third of the orange mousse. Place the second layer of sponge on top and brush lightly with sugar syrup. Put the remaining orange segments onto the surface and cover with a layer of orange mousse.

Position the third layer of sponge on top and brush with sugar syrup. Spread the remaining mousse over the surface of the cake. Chill overnight prior to use.

To serve, remove the cake collar by running a hot sharp knife around the edge, then carefully ease the collar upwards. Decorate the side of the cake with finely chopped toasted pistachio nuts. Decorate the top with the candied julienned orange peel.

RASPBERRY AND WHITE CHOCOLATE MUFFINS

These delicious, pretty muffins, dusted with confectioner's sugar, are ideal to serve as a snack.
Blueberries may replace the raspberries.

MAKES 9 LARGE MUFFINS

- 2 cups all-purpose flour
- 1 tablespoon baking powder
- 4½ oz superfine sugar
- 1 cup milk
- ¼ cup butter, melted and slightly cooled
- 1 large egg, beaten
- 1 cup chopped white chocolate
- 2 cups fresh or frozen raspberries (see Tip)
- ½ cup flaked almonds
- Pure confectioner's sugar, for dusting

Preheat the oven to 375°F. Butter nine large muffin cups, or line the cups with paper liners.

Sift the flour and baking powder into a large bowl. Stir in the sugar.

Combine the milk, melted butter and egg and add to the dry ingredients. Using a rubber spatula, fold in until just combined (do no overmix), then fold in the chopped chocolate and raspberries.

Divide the mixture among the prepared muffin cups. Sprinkle each muffin with flaked almonds.

Bake for 20–25 minutes, or until firm on top and golden; note that these muffins are still quite moist when cooked, so testing with a skewer is not the most accurate method. Allow to cool for 5 minutes in the pan, then transfer to a wire rack. Dust with confectioner's sugar and serve warm or cold.

Tip
- If using frozen raspberries, there is no need to thaw them first.

MERINGUE ROLL WITH WHITE CHOCOLATE PASSIONFRUIT CREAM

SERVES 8

MERINGUE ROLL
6 large egg whites ▪
7 oz superfine sugar, ▪
plus about 1 tablespoon extra, for dusting
1 teaspoon natural vanilla extract ▪
1½ teaspoons cornstarch ▪
1½ teaspoons white vinegar ▪
1 tablespoon sugar mixed with ½ teaspoon ground cinnamon ▪
⅔ cup slivered almonds ▪

PASSIONFRUIT CREAM
1¼ cups whipping cream ▪
Pulp of 4–6 fresh passionfruit ▪
¾ cup chopped white chocolate, ▪
melted and cooled

Preheat the oven to 350°F. Butter a 9 x 13 inch shallow cake pan or baking sheet and line it with parchment paper, extending the paper about 2 inches over the long sides of the pan. Butter the parchment paper well.

MERINGUE ROLL
Using an electric mixer, beat the egg whites in a large bowl until soft peaks form. Add the sugar gradually, beating on medium–high speed, for 2–3 minutes, or until the mixture is thick and glossy, and the sugar has dissolved. Fold in the vanilla, cornflour, and vinegar.

Pour into the prepared pan and smooth the surface. Sprinkle with the cinnamon sugar and slivered almonds. Bake for 15–18 minutes, or until firm to the touch. Allow to cool in the pan for 10 minutes.

Cover a wire rack with a sheet of parchment paper. Turn the meringue out onto the paper. Carefully peel away the paper on the bottom of the meringue while it is warm. Use the paper on the wire rack to gently roll up the meringue lengthways. Leave until cool.

PASSIONFRUIT CREAM
Whip the cream until stiff peaks form. Add the passionfruit pulp, then stir in the cooled white chocolate. Do not over-mix.

Carefully unroll the meringue. Spread it with the passionfruit cream and roll it up again, using the paper to assist you. Place on a serving platter and remove the paper. Refrigerate until firm, then slice thickly to serve.

FILLING VARIATIONS

MANGO
Fold diced fresh mango (1 large or 2 small mangoes) into the whipped cream before adding the cooled white chocolate.

PEACH
Add poached fresh peaches, drained and diced, to the whipped cream before adding the cooled white chocolate.

APRICOT
Add poached fresh apricots, drained and diced, to the whipped cream before adding the cooled white chocolate.

COFFEE CHOCOLATE CREAM
Sift together 2 teaspoons unsweetened cocoa powder, 2 teaspoons instant coffee granules and 2 teaspoons pure confectioner's sugar and add to the unwhipped cream. Allow to stand for 1 hour before whipping, then fold in ⅔ cup chopped dark chocolate that has been melted and cooled (instead of the white chocolate).

CHOCOLATE CHIP
Omit the white chocolate from the filling and add ¾ cup grated dark chocolate to the whipped cream. Serve with Cherry Sauce (page 231).

PLUM UPSIDE-DOWN CAKE

Any type of plum may be used for this cake, although blood plums have an especially attractive color.
Yellow peaches, apricots or peeled and quartered pears may replace the plums.

SERVES 12

TOPPING
⅓ cup unsalted butter, melted ▪
½ cup lightly packed soft brown sugar ▪
1 teaspoon ground cinnamon ▪
10–12 ripe plums, halved and pitted ▪

CAKE
1 cup unsalted butter, at room temperature ▪
7 oz superfine sugar ▪
4 large eggs, lightly beaten ▪
1⅔ cups all-purpose flour ▪
1⅔ cups self-rising flour ▪
¾ cup milk ▪
1 cup ground almonds or ground hazelnuts ▪
1 cup chopped dark chocolate ▪

Preheat the oven to 375°F. Butter a 10 inch round cake pan.

TOPPING
Pour the melted butter into the prepared cake pan. Sprinkle the brown sugar and cinnamon over the top. Arrange the plums, cut side down, over the topping, working from the outside to the center.

CAKE
Using an electric mixer, cream the butter and sugar until pale and fluffy. Gradually add the eggs, mixing well after each addition.

Sift the flours together and fold gently into the creamed mixture alternately with the milk.

Spoon half the mixture into the cake pan. Sprinkle over the ground almonds or hazelnuts and chopped chocolate. Spoon over the remaining mixture and smooth the surface.

Bake for 55–60 minutes, or until a skewer inserted into the center of the cake comes out clean.

Allow to cool in the pan for 5 minutes, then carefully turn out onto a serving platter. Serve warm or cold with cream or ice cream.

Tip
▪ This recipe is best made on the day of serving.

WHITE CHOCOLATE BANANA CAKE

This simple but impressive-looking cake, decorated elaborately with chocolate curls, makes an ideal birthday cake. Chopped walnuts may be added to the base mix.

SERVES 8–10

Preheat the oven to 350°F. Butter two 8 inch cake pans and line them with parchment paper.

CAKE
3 large ripe bananas ■
3 large eggs ■
1 cup superfine sugar ■
1 teaspoon natural vanilla extract ■
½ cup vegetable oil ■
2 cups self-rising flour ■
1 teaspoon baking soda ■
1⅓ cups roughly chopped white chocolate ■

FILLING, TOPPING AND DECORATION
1¼ cups whipping cream ■
2 large ripe bananas ■
1 teaspoon natural vanilla extract or dark rum ■
Lemon juice, for dipping bananas ■
White chocolate curls or rolls (page 233) ■

CAKE
Mash the bananas in a large bowl.

Whisk the eggs, sugar and vanilla extract, and stir into the mashed bananas along with the oil.

Sift the flour and baking soda together. Using a rubber spatula, fold into the banana mixture. Fold in the chopped chocolate until well combined.

Pour the mixture into the prepared pans. Bake for about 30 minutes, or until a skewer inserted into the center of the cake comes out clean. Allow to cool in the pans on a wire rack for 10 minutes, then turn out onto the wire rack to cool completely.

FILLING, TOPPING AND DECORATION
Whip the cream until stiff peaks form. Mash one of the bananas in a separate bowl and add half of the whipped cream. Add the vanilla extract or rum.

To assemble, spread one cake with the banana cream. Place the second cake on top and spread the surface with the remaining cream. Slice the last banana, then dip the slices in lemon juice to prevent them from browning. Decorate the cake with banana slices and chocolate curls.

chapter five

NUTS ABOUT CHOCOLATE

Hazelnut and chocolate, macadamia and chocolate, almond and chocolate, pecan and chocolate—all are delightful flavor combinations. Chopped or ground nuts folded through sublime chocolate cakes add a heavenly flavor dimension, extra richness, and an interesting contrast of texture.

CHOCOLATE PISTACHIO WAFER BREAD

Serve these wafers as a delicious and decorative addition to ice cream, or as an accompaniment to a fruit and cheese platter.
The loaf can be made the day before it is sliced and dried.

MAKES ABOUT 35

1⅓ cups all-purpose flour ▪
⅓ cup unsweetened cocoa powder, ▪
preferably Dutch style
6 large egg whites ▪
1 cup superfine sugar ▪
1 cup unsalted pistachio nuts ▪

Preheat the oven to 300°F. Butter a 5 x 9 inch loaf pan and line it with parchment paper.

Sift the flour and cocoa powder together.

Using an electric mixer, beat the egg whites until soft peaks form. Gradually add the sugar to the egg whites and continue beating for 2–3 minutes, or until the sugar is dissolved and the mixture forms a thick meringue. Do not overbeat.

Using a rubber spatula, lightly fold the sifted dry ingredients into the meringue, then fold in the pistachio nuts.

Pour the mixture into the prepared pan. Bake for 45–50 minutes, or until cooked when tested with a skewer. Allow to cool in the pan on a wire rack.

Slice the cold loaf very thinly with a sharp serrated knife. Put the slices on baking sheets and allow to dry, without coloring, in a 275°F oven for 15–20 minutes. Turn the slices and bake for a further 15–20 minutes. Transfer to a wire rack; the slices will harden and become crisp as they cool.

Store in an airtight container.

Tip
▪ To intensify the color of the pistachios, blanch them in boiling water, drain immediately, and spread on a sheet of paper towel to absorb moisture. Peel the excess skins from the nuts.

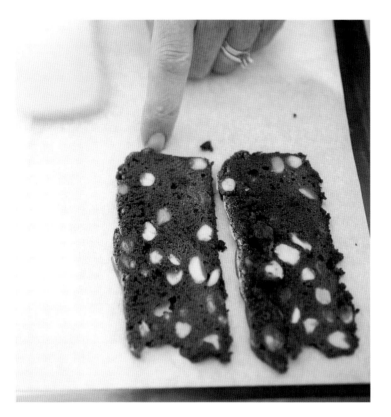

ALMOND AND CHOCOLATE TUILES

Tuiles are elegant, lacy wafers to accompany desserts, or in which to serve ice cream.
Use smaller rounds if making them as a cookie accompaniment.

MAKES 14–16

2 large eggs ■
½ cup pure confectioner's sugar ■
½ cup all-purpose flour ■
½ oz unsweetened cocoa powder, ■
preferably Dutch style
⅓ cup flaked almonds ■
¼ cup unsalted butter, melted and cooled ■

Preheat the oven to 350°F. Line 2 baking sheets with parchment paper.

Beat the eggs lightly in a bowl until just broken up.

Sift the sugar, then add gradually to the eggs. Using a hand whisk or a fork, mix gently; do not aerate the mixture.

Sift the flour and cocoa powder into the egg mixture and fold in using a rubber spatula. Add the flaked almonds and cooled melted butter, and stir well.

Making two tuiles per sheet, drop small spoonfuls of mixture onto the prepared sheets, allowing room for spreading. Using a small spatula, spread each spoonful of mixture out very thinly to form a disc 4½ inches in diameter.

Bake, one tray at a time, for 5–6 minutes, until the edges of the tuiles feel firm. Lift the cookies carefully with a spatula and, while still warm, place them over a rolling pin or a glass lying on its side. This gives the tuiles their characteristic shape.

Leave for 2 minutes, or until set, then transfer to a wire rack to cool completely. As soon as they are cool, store in an airtight container.

MERINGUE NUT CAKE

The nuts can be varied in this meringue cake. Use one type, or mix them up; pecans, macadamia nuts, and almonds combine well. This cake is delicious served with fresh raspberries.

SERVES 10–12

8 large eggs, separated ■
1/2 cup brandy ■
1 2/3 cups superfine sugar ■
1/4 teaspoon cream of tartar ■
2 cups finely chopped walnuts ■
1 2/3 cups toasted, skinned and ■
finely chopped hazelnuts (see Notes)

FILLING
1 1/4 cups whipping cream ■
2–3 tablespoons dark rum, to taste ■
2 cups chopped dark or milk chocolate, ■
melted and cooled to tepid

Preheat the oven to 315°F. Butter and flour a 10 inch springform pan. Line it with parchment paper, then butter the paper well.

Put the egg yolks, brandy and half the sugar in a bowl. Using an electric mixer, beat for about 3 minutes, or until thick and pale, and ribbons form when the beaters are lifted out of the mixture.

In the bowl of an electric mixer, beat the egg whites and cream of tartar on high speed until soft peaks form. Beat in the remaining sugar gradually and continue beating until stiff peaks form, and the mixture is thick and glossy, 4–5 minutes.

Using a rubber spatula, fold the meringue mixture into the egg-yolk mixture in two batches. Lightly fold in the chopped nuts. Pour into the prepared cake pan, spreading gently with a spatula.

Bake for 1 1/4 hours, or until the meringue is firm. Allow to cool in the pan, then remove the side of the pan and peel off the parchment paper.

FILLING
Beat the cream until stiff peaks form, then stir in the rum and tepid melted chocolate.

To assemble, cut the meringue in half horizontally. Spread the filling on one half of the cake and top with the second meringue half.

NOTES To toast nuts, put them in a single layer on a baking tray and bake in a preheated 350°F oven for 5–10 minutes, depending on the type of nut. Stir occasionally with a wooden spoon to aid even toasting, and keep an eye on them, as they can burn easily.

To remove the skins from toasted hazelnuts, tip the hot nuts into a clean dish towel, gather up the corners, and rub the parcel vigorously to loosen the skins. Not all of the skins will come off; do not worry about those that don't.

Nuts can be ground in a food processor; allow toasted nuts to cool completely before being ground.

NUTTY CHOCOLATE CAKE

A variety of nuts can be used in this recipe; use one type only, or mix two or more as you choose.
Bake the cake the day before you need it; the flavor will mellow and it will be easier to slice.

SERVES 10

1 cup chopped dark chocolate ■
2 teaspoons orange juice or orange liqueur (optional) ■
Finely grated zest of ½ orange ■
½ cup unsalted butter, diced ■
3 large eggs ■
½ cup superfine sugar ■
1 teaspoon natural vanilla extract ■
½ cup cornstarch ■
1 tablespoon self-rising flour ■
1 cup roughly chopped unsalted pecans, ■
almonds, pistachio nuts, and/or macadamia nuts

1 quantity Easy Chocolate Glaze (page 226; optional) ■
Extra unsalted nuts, for decoration (optional) ■

Preheat the oven to 350°F. Butter a 8 inch round cake pan and line it with parchment paper.

Combine the chocolate, orange juice or liqueur, and orange zest in a heatproof bowl over hot water, ensuring that the base of the bowl does not touch the water. Heat, stirring, until the chocolate is melted and the mixture is combined, then whisk in the butter, one piece at a time, until the mixture is smooth.

Using an electric mixer, beat together the eggs, sugar and vanilla extract for about 3 minutes, or until thickened. Sift the cornstarch and flour together, then fold into the egg mixture.

Using a rubber spatula, gently fold this mixture into the chocolate mixture. Fold in the chopped nuts.

Pour the mixture into the prepared pan. Bake for about 35 minutes, or until cooked when tested with a skewer. Allow to cool in the pan on a wire rack for 10 minutes, then turn out onto the wire rack and allow to cool completely.

Pour the glaze over the top of the cooled cake and smooth with a metal spatula. Decorate with extra nuts if desired.

VARIATION
COFFEE
1 tablespoon freshly brewed espresso coffee or coffee liqueur can replace the orange juice or zest, and orange liqueur.

WHITE CHOCOLATE MACADAMIA SHORTBREAD

Due to the white chocolate that it contains, this recipe has a softer texture than traditional shortbread.

MAKES 24

1 cup unsalted butter, chopped ▪
½ cup lightly packed soft dark brown sugar ▪
⅔ cup pure confectioner's sugar, sifted ▪
1 teaspoon natural vanilla extract ▪
2 cups all-purpose flour ▪
⅓ cup cornstarch ▪
¾ cup chopped white chocolate ▪
1 cup chopped unsalted macadamia nuts ▪
1 tablespoon superfine sugar ▪

Preheat the oven to 325°F. Butter a 9 x 13 inch cake pan and line it with parchment paper, extending the paper over two sides of the pan to allow for easy removal later.

Using an electric mixer, beat the butter until pale, then add the sugars and vanilla extract. Continue beating until pale and fluffy.

Sift the flour and cornstarch together. Add to the creamed mixture and beat lightly until the mixture just comes together.

Add the chopped chocolate and nuts. Using a wooden spoon, work them through the mixture.

Using lightly floured hands, press the mixture into the prepared pan. Mark into rectangles using the back of a knife and sprinkle with the superfine sugar.

Bake for 30–35 minutes, until a light golden color. Allow to cool completely in the pan on a wire rack, then remove from the pan and cut into rectangles. Store in an airtight container.

CHOCOLATE ALMOND BISCOTTI

Sweet, dry, and crisp, biscotti are ideal to serve with coffee or ice cream—or, in the traditional Italian manner, with a dessert wine such as Vin Santo.

MAKES ABOUT 30

3¼ cups almonds ▪
3 cups all-purpose flour ▪
3 cups self-rising flour ▪
2¼ cups superfine sugar ▪
3⅓ cups chopped dark chocolate, melted and cooled ▪
5 large eggs, lightly beaten ▪
1 teaspoon natural vanilla extract ▪

Preheat the oven to 335°F. Lightly butter baking sheets (you will need three small or two large sheets).

Put the almonds on another baking tray and bake for 6–8 minutes, stirring occasionally, until lightly toasted. Allow to cool.

Sift the flours together into a large mixing bowl. Add the sugar, cooled toasted almonds, melted chocolate, eggs and vanilla extract. Using your hands, mix to a stiff dough.

Divide the dough into three portions and roll each portion into a log about 2 inches in diameter and 12 inches long.

Place the logs on the baking sheets, allowing room for spreading, and bake for 20–30 minutes, or until brown.

Transfer to a wire rack and allow to cool completely (this prevents them from crumbling when sliced). Using a serrated knife, cut into ⅝ inch slices. Return to the trays and bake in a preheated 200°F oven for 15–20 minutes. Transfer to a wire rack; the biscotti will harden and become crisp as they cool. Store in an airtight container.

VARIATIONS

JAFFA
Add 2 tablespoons chopped candied orange peel.

WHITE CHOCOLATE
Substitute white chocolate for dark. A nice addition to the white chocolate version is 2 tablespoons dried cranberries; add them at the same time as the almonds.

CHOCOLATE PECAN PIE

*A dear friend, June Blanchett, arrived at my door with a piping hot pecan pie on the evening
that my family moved into a new house. I have adapted her recipe to make a chocolate version.*

SERVES 10

PASTRY PIE SHELL
1⅓ cups all-purpose flour ▪
⅔ cup pure confectioner's sugar ▪
⅓ cup ground almonds ▪
2½ oz unsalted butter, chopped ▪
1 large egg, beaten ▪
⅓ cup chopped dark chocolate ▪

PIE FILLING
2 cups pecans ▪
7¾ fl oz light corn syrup ▪
⅓ cup firmly packed soft brown sugar ▪
3¼ oz white sugar ▪
¼ cup unsalted butter, chopped ▪
⅔ cup chopped dark chocolate, melted ▪
4 large eggs, beaten ▪
1 teaspoon natural vanilla extract ▪
½ cup flaked almonds (optional) ▪

Lightly butter a deep, loose-based 10 inch round tart pan or a deep baking dish.

PASTRY PIE SHELL
Sift the flour and confectioner's sugar into a bowl, add the ground almonds and rub in the butter until the mixture resembles breadcrumbs.

Add the egg and mix together to form a soft dough. Turn out onto a lightly floured board and knead lightly. Wrap in plastic wrap and refrigerate for 30 minutes.

Roll the pastry out thinly between two sheets of parchment paper or plastic wrap and use it to line the tart pan. The pastry will be soft; if any holes form, patch them with scraps of pastry. Refrigerate for 2–3 hours to firm, then trim the edge of the pastry.

Preheat the oven to 350°F.

Line the pastry shell with a piece of crumpled parchment paper and pour in some baking beads, dried beans or uncooked rice. Bake for 10 minutes. Remove the paper and beads and bake for a further 10 minutes. Allow to cool in the tart pan, then melt the chocolate and brush it over the cooled pie shell.

PIE FILLING
Line the base of the pie shell with the pecans.

Put the corn syrup and sugars in a saucepan and bring to a boil. Remove from the heat. Whisk in the butter and hot melted chocolate. Gradually pour the hot syrup mixture into the eggs, whisking constantly; this helps to thicken the mixture. Stir in the vanilla extract and allow to cool.

Fill the pie shell with the cooled filling and sprinkle with flaked almonds, if using. Bake for 40 minutes, or until golden in color and almost set. (Note that the filling will not set entirely until it has cooled.) Serve hot or cold with cream or ice cream.

VARIATION
1 tablespoon Bourbon may be added to the filling mix.

CHOCOLATE MACADAMIA CAKE

This is a sophisticated, rich, moist European-style cake.
It can be decorated with macadamia nuts dipped in chocolate, and chocolate leaves.

SERVES 10

CAKE
1 cup unsalted macadamia nuts ■
1²/₃ cups chopped dark chocolate ■
2 tablespoons instant coffee granules ■
2 tablespoons hot water ■
4 large eggs, separated ■
1 cup unsalted butter, at room temperature ■
½ cup superfine sugar ■
⅓ cup cornstarch ■
¼ teaspoon cream of tartar ■

CHOCOLATE GLAZE
1¼ cups chopped dark chocolate ■
⅓ cup freshly brewed espresso coffee ■

Preheat the oven to 350°F. Butter a 9 inch round cake pan and line it with parchment paper.

CAKE
Put the macadamia nuts on a baking sheet and toast in the oven for 5–7 minutes, or until golden. Set aside until cool enough to handle, then chop finely.

Put the chocolate, coffee granules and hot water in a heatproof bowl over a saucepan of hot water and heat gently until the chocolate is melted. Remove from the heat.

Beat in the egg yolks one at a time. Replace the bowl over the saucepan of hot water and heat, stirring, for 1–2 minutes, until the mixture thickens. Remove from the heat and beat in the butter until it is melted, and the mixture is smooth and glossy.

Mix the macadamia nuts, half the sugar and the cornstarch together, then beat into the chocolate mixture. Allow to cool.

Beat the egg whites, cream of tartar, and remaining sugar on high speed for 3 minutes, or until stiff peaks form. Using a rubber spatula, fold gently into the chocolate mixture.

Pour the mixture into the prepared pan and bake for 35–40 minutes, or until a skewer inserted into the center of the cake comes out clean. Allow to cool in the pan before turning out.

CHOCOLATE GLAZE
Put the chocolate and hot coffee in a heatproof bowl over a saucepan of hot water, and heat gently until the chocolate is melted. Cool until the mixture is of a spreadable consistency, then spread evenly over the top and side of the cake.

THE ULTIMATE TRUFFLE BROWNIE

Brownies are an American icon. Their exact origins are unknown, but folklore theory is that someone once forgot to include the leavening agent when baking a cake. The rest is history.

MAKES ABOUT 32

1 cup unsalted butter ■
2²/₃ cups chopped dark chocolate ■
2¼ cups superfine sugar ■
4 large eggs, beaten ■
2 teaspoons natural vanilla extract ■
1½ cups all-purpose flour ■
2 tablespoons unsweetened cocoa powder, ■
preferably Dutch style
1⅓ cups hazelnuts, toasted, ■
skins removed, chopped

CHOCOLATE TRUFFLE GLAZE
½ cup whipping cream ■
1⅓ cups finely chopped dark chocolate ■

Preheat the oven to 350°F. Butter a 9 x 13 inch cake pan and line it with parchment paper, extending the paper over two sides of the pan to allow for easy removal later.

In a large saucepan over low heat, melt the butter. Remove from the heat, add the chocolate, allow to stand for 2 minutes, then stir until smooth. Allow to cool.

Using a wire whisk or electric beaters, whisk the sugar, beaten eggs and vanilla until thickened. Stir into the chocolate mixture.

Sift together the flour and cocoa powder. Using a rubber spatula, fold into the chocolate mixture. Fold in the hazelnuts.

Pour the mixture into the prepared pan. Bake for 30–35 minutes, until the surface forms a crust (note that brownies are very moist, so testing them with a skewer will not give an accurate result). Allow to cool completely in the pan on a wire rack.

CHOCOLATE TRUFFLE GLAZE
Bring the cream to a boil in a small saucepan. Remove from the heat. Add the chocolate and stir until smooth. Allow to cool to a spreadable consistency.

Spread the cooled chocolate glaze over the surface of the cake. Allow to set. To serve, cut into squares using a hot, dry knife. Store in an airtight container.

VARIATION
Toasted unsalted walnuts, pecans, or macadamia nuts can be substituted for hazelnuts.

ALMOND FRANGIPANE TART

Frangipane is a creamy almond filling for cakes and pastries. In this recipe, it is laced with rum and dark chocolate.
Finely chopped candied ginger could be added for flavor variation.

SERVES 6–8

1 quantity Sweet Pie Pastry (page 32) ▪

FRANGIPANE
½ cup unsalted butter, at room temperature ▪
½ cup superfine sugar ▪
2 large eggs, beaten ▪
⅔ cup finely chopped dark chocolate ▪
1 tablespoon dark rum ▪
1¼ cups ground almonds ▪
½ cup flaked almonds ▪

Pure confectioner's sugar, for dusting (optional) ▪

Preheat the oven to 325°F. Lightly butter an 8 inch loose-based tart pan.

FRANGIPANE
Using an electric mixer, beat the butter until pale. Add the sugar, and continue beating until pale and fluffy.

Add the eggs gradually, mixing well after each addition. Add the chocolate and rum, then stir in the ground almonds.

To make the tart, roll out the pastry to a thickness of about ¼ inch and use it to line the tart pan. (There will be some pastry left over.) Refrigerate for 30 minutes to firm, then trim the edge of the pastry, and fill the uncooked tart case with the frangipane filling. Sprinkle over the flaked almonds. Bake for 45 minutes, or until golden brown.

Cool in the pan on a wire rack for 10 minutes, then remove from the pan and leave on the wire rack to cool completely.

Serve dusted with confectioner's sugar, if desired.

VARIATION
Ground hazelnuts can replace the ground almonds.

Tip
▪ Use the frangipane at room temperature. It may be refrigerated for up to three days, or frozen for up to one month; allow to return to room temperature before using.

FLOURLESS HAZELNUT CHOCOLATE CAKE

Hazelnut and chocolate is such a superb flavor combination that the Italians have given it its own name—gianduia.

SERVES 12

CAKE
2 cups chopped dark chocolate ■
⅓ cup unsalted butter ■
7 large eggs, separated ■
½ teaspoon cream of tartar ■
½ cup superfine sugar ■
¾ cup ground hazelnuts ■

CHOCOLATE GLAZE
1⅓ cups chopped dark chocolate ■
½ cup unsalted butter ■

4 tablespoons chopped toasted hazelnuts, to decorate ■

Preheat the oven to 315°F. Butter a 9 inch springform pan or deep round cake pan and line it with parchment paper.

CAKE
Melt the chocolate and butter gently in a heatproof bowl over hot water, ensuring that the base of the bowl does not touch the water. Remove from the heat and allow to cool.

Using an electric mixer, beat the egg yolks for 1–2 minutes, or until pale and thick, and ribbons form when the beaters are lifted out of the mixture.

Using clean beaters, beat the egg whites and cream of tartar in a large bowl until soft peaks form. Gradually beat in the sugar, then continue beating until the mixture is stiff but not dry.

Combine the egg yolks and melted chocolate mixture and beat gently. Using a rubber spatula, fold half the meringue into the chocolate mixture, then return this combined mixture to the remaining meringue. Add the ground hazelnuts and fold in gently until combined.

Pour into the prepared pan and bake for 50–55 minutes, or until the cake comes away slightly from the side of the pan. Allow to cool completely in the pan before turning out.

CHOCOLATE GLAZE
Combine the chocolate, butter, and 2 tablespoons water in a heatproof bowl over hot water. Stir until smooth. Allow to cool, then spread over the top and side of the cake.

Decorate side edge of the cake by pressing the chopped toasted hazelnuts into the glaze.

VARIATION
Combine 2 tablespoons coffee liqueur, and 2 tablespoons espresso or freshly brewed, cooled strong coffee. Add to the recipe along with the ground hazelnuts.

MACADAMIA AND CRANBERRY COOKIES

Sweetened dried cranberries—sometimes marketed as craisins—give a chewy texture to these white-chocolate-studded cookies.

MAKES 30 LARGE OR 60 SMALL COOKIES

1 cup unsalted butter, at room temperature ■
3/4 cup firmly packed dark brown sugar ■
1/2 cup superfine sugar ■
2 large eggs ■
1 teaspoon natural vanilla extract ■
2 1/2 cups all-purpose flour ■
1 teaspoon baking soda ■
1 1/2 cups coarsely chopped unsalted macadamia nuts ■
2 1/4 cups coarsely chopped white chocolate ■
1 cup sweetened dried cranberries ■

Preheat the oven to 325°F. Lightly butter two baking sheets or line them with parchment paper.

Using an electric mixer, beat the butter, brown sugar and superfine sugar until pale and fluffy. Whisk the eggs and vanilla extract, then gradually beat into the creamed butter mixture.

Sift the flour and baking soda into the egg mixture, and mix until combined. Stir in the nuts, chocolate, and cranberries.

Place spoonfuls of mixture onto the sheets, allowing room for spreading. Dip a fork into cold water and use the back of the tines to flatten the top of each cookie.

Bake for 12–15 minutes for small cookies, or 15–18 minutes for large, or until golden in color. Allow to cool for 5 minutes on the tray, then transfer the cookies to a wire rack and allow to firm.

Store in an airtight container.

WHITE CHOCOLATE BROWNIES
WITH CHOCOLATE CHUNKS

MAKES 18

BROWNIES
1 cup unsalted butter ▪
1¾ cups chopped white chocolate ▪
3 large eggs ▪
9 oz superfine sugar ▪
1 teaspoon natural vanilla extract ▪
1 tablespoon light corn syrup (optional; see Note) ▪
3 cups all-purpose flour ▪
1 cup roughly chopped dark chocolate ▪
1 cup roughly chopped unsalted ▪
pecans or walnuts

CHOCOLATE GLAZE
4 tablespoons whipping cream ▪
1 cup finely chopped white chocolate ▪
1 teaspoon light corn syrup or unsalted butter ▪

Preheat the oven to 350°F. Butter a 12 x 16 inch cake pan and line it with parchment paper, extending the paper over two sides of the pan to allow for easy removal later.

BROWNIES
Melt the butter in a saucepan over low heat. Remove from the heat, add half the chopped white chocolate, and stir until smooth.

Using a hand whisk or an electric mixer, beat the eggs, sugar, vanilla extract and corn syrup, if using, in a small bowl until well combined. Carefully stir in the white chocolate mixture.

Sift the flour, fold it into the mixture, then fold in the remaining chopped chocolate (both white and dark) and the chopped nuts.

Spread the mixture evenly in the prepared pan. Bake for 30 minutes, or until firm on top and golden. If the mixture begins to brown too much, cover it loosely with a sheet of foil.

Allow to cool completely in the pan on a wire rack.

CHOCOLATE GLAZE
Bring the cream to a boil in a small saucepan, then remove from the heat. Add the chocolate and corn syrup or butter. Allow to stand for 3 minutes, stir, then allow to cool. Once cool, pour the glaze over the brownie slab. When the glaze is set, remove the brownie slab from the pan, and cut into squares.

Store in an airtight container.

Tips
▪ If you don't have light corn syrup, simply omit it; it makes the texture a little more fudgy, but is not essential.
▪ Allow the brownies to cool completely before you eat them; or better still, make them the day before you intend to serve them.

HAZELNUT PRALINE CAKE

Crunchy caramelized hazelnuts add flavor to this cake, which is filled with milk chocolate cream. Almonds can replace hazelnuts in both the praline and the cake.

SERVES 10–12

½ quantity Nut Praline (page 112), made with hazelnuts; ■
break some of the praline into shards for decoration,
and crush the rest

CAKE
6 large eggs, separated ■
½ cup superfine sugar, ■
plus 1 tablespoon extra
1¼ cups chopped dark chocolate, ■
melted and cooled to tepid
1⅔ cups ground hazelnuts ■

MILK CHOCOLATE CREAM
1½ cups whipping cream ■
2 cups finely chopped milk chocolate ■
¼ cup unsalted butter ■

Preheat the oven to 350°F. Butter two 9 inch round cake pans or one 10 inch round cake pan, and line with parchment paper.

CAKE
Using an electric mixer, beat the egg yolks and the ½ cup sugar on medium–high speed until pale and thickened.

Using clean beaters, beat the egg whites until soft peaks form. Add the 1 tablespoon superfine sugar and beat until the mixture is glossy.

Mix the tepid chocolate with 3 tablespoons water, and add to the egg-yolk mixture. Using a rubber spatula, fold in the hazelnuts. Gently fold in the meringue in two batches, until combined.

Pour the mixture into the prepared pan(s). Bake for 30–35 minutes, or until the top is firm to the touch. Allow to cool completely in the pan(s) before turning out.

MILK CHOCOLATE CREAM
Bring the cream to a boil in a saucepan. Remove from the heat. Add the chocolate, allow to stand for 1 minute, then stir until smooth. Allow to cool slightly, then stir in the butter. Cover and chill for 2 hours.

Using a wooden spoon, beat the chilled mixture until thickened.

ASSEMBLY
Slice each of the 9 inch cakes horizontally into two layers, or the 10 inch cake horizontally into three layers. Put one cake layer on a cake board and, using a spatula dipped in hot water then dried, spread with some of the milk chocolate cream. Sprinkle with some of the crushed praline, then top with another cake layer. Repeat this process until all the layers have been assembled.

Spread the remaining chocolate cream on the top and side of the cake. Sprinkle the surface with crushed praline, and decorate with shards of praline.

Cover the cake lightly and refrigerate until ready to serve.

NUT PRALINE

Praline is a type of nut toffee that can either be crushed finely and incorporated into other mixtures, or broken into decorative shards. Various nuts can be used.

MAKES ABOUT 2 LB 4 OZ

2 cups superfine sugar ▪
3¼ cups unsalted nuts (blanched almonds, ▪
skinned hazelnuts, roughly chopped macadamia nuts,
or pistachio nuts), warmed

Lightly brush a large baking sheet (or a marble slab, if you have one) with vegetable oil.

Put the sugar and 3½ fl oz water in a heavy-based saucepan. Stir to combine. Bring to a boil and cook, without stirring, until a light caramel color develops, or the mixture reaches 235°F on a sugar thermometer (soft-ball stage; see Note, page 204). To prevent crystallization, brush down the side of the pan from time to time with a pastry brush dipped in water.

Add the nuts and stir over low heat with a metal spatula. When the sugar begins to caramelize, increase the heat and continue to cook, without stirring, until the mixture is a deep honey color.

Pour the mixture over the oiled baking sheet or marble slab. Allow to cool and harden.

Once set, break the praline into shards, or crush with a rolling pin. Store the shards or crushed praline in an airtight container in a cool, dry place. It can be frozen to prevent it from becoming sticky.

NUTS ABOUT CHOCOLATE

WHITE CHOCOLATE ALMOND SQUARES

This moist bar is delicious on its own, or frosted and sprinkled with toasted chopped nuts for a special occasion. It looks lovely topped with a glaze or ganache, decorated with crystallized violets, arranged into a pyramid, and decorated with fresh violets.

MAKES 18

1¼ cups chopped white chocolate ▪
¾ cup unsalted butter ▪
4 large eggs, separated ▪
1 teaspoon natural vanilla extract ▪
¾ cup superfine sugar ▪
1 cup ground almonds or ground hazelnuts ▪
½ cup all-purpose flour ▪
¼ teaspoon cream of tartar ▪

½ quantity Rich Chocolate Glaze (page 226), ▪
made with white chocolate (optional)
Pure confectioner's sugar, for dusting (optional) ▪

Preheat the oven to 350°F. Butter a 9 x 13 inch cake pan and line it with parchment paper, extending the paper over two sides of the pan to allow for easy removal later.

Melt the chocolate and butter in a heatproof bowl over hot water. Stir until smooth and allow to cool until tepid.

Using an electric mixer, beat the egg yolks and vanilla extract with ½ cup of the sugar until thickened and pale, about 2 minutes. Stir this mixture into the tepid chocolate mixture, along with the nuts and sifted flour. Set aside.

Using clean, dry beaters, beat the egg whites and cream of tartar until stiff peaks form, then continue to beat while gradually adding the remaining sugar. Beat for 2–3 minutes, or until the sugar is dissolved and a meringue forms. Using a rubber spatula, fold the meringue gently into the chocolate mixture in two batches.

Pour the mixture into the prepared pan. Bake for 30 minutes, or until cooked when tested with a skewer.

Allow to cool completely in the pan on a wire rack. Remove from the pan, cut into squares and frost with the glaze if desired, or dust with sifted confectioner's sugar.

chapter six

COOL CHOCOLATE

From ice cream, sorbet, semifreddo, and frozen terrines, silky smooth crème brûlée, and panna cotta, to extravagant meringue tortes, cheesecakes, and mousses— chilled and frozen chocolate desserts offer a decadent and sumptuous way to round off a meal, especially on a summer's day.

CLASSIC CHOCOLATE ICE CREAM

*Made in the classic French way, with a cooked egg-custard base, this ice cream
is delicious just as it is, but also easily lends itself to many tempting variations.*

MAKES ABOUT 6 CUPS

2 cups whole milk ■
1 2/3 cups finely chopped dark chocolate ■
1 vanilla bean, split, seeds removed and reserved (the pod can ■
be kept for another use; see page 17)
9 oz white sugar ■
5 large egg yolks ■
2 tablespoons unsweetened cocoa powder, ■
preferably Dutch style
2 cups whipping cream ■

Heat the milk, chocolate, vanilla seeds, and half the sugar in a saucepan over low heat until just boiling. Stir until the chocolate has melted.

Using an electric mixer, beat the egg yolks, sifted cocoa powder, and the remaining sugar in a bowl. Slowly pour the hot milk over the egg mixture, stirring constantly with a wooden spoon, then return the mixture to the cleaned saucepan. Heat over low heat, stirring constantly, until the mixture thickens and coats the back of the wooden spoon. Remove from the heat and strain into a large bowl. Add the cream and stir well. Cover with plastic wrap and refrigerate for 4 hours, or until chilled.

Churn in an ice-cream machine according to the manufacturer's instructions; depending on the capacity of your machine, you may need to do this in two batches. Alternatively, freeze in metal trays. If using trays, beat the mixture once it reaches the point of freezing to increase the volume, then return to the freezer.

VARIATIONS

CHOCOLATE HAZELNUT OR PECAN
Add 3/4 cup chopped toasted unsalted hazelnuts, or roughly chopped pecans once the ice cream is fully churned; then churn again briefly just to combine.

CHOCOLATE PRALINE
Add about 3/4 cup crushed Nut Praline (page 112) after the base mixture has been refrigerated, and before it is churned.

CHOCOLATE LIQUEUR
Add 2 tablespoons of the liqueur of your choice to the base mixture before churning.

CHOCOLATE APRICOT
Add 2/3 cup dried apricots, finely chopped and soaked in 2 tablespoons brandy for 2–3 hours, to the base mixture before churning.

CHOCOLATE BANANA
Add 1 cup of mashed banana, along with the juice of 1/2 lemon, to the base mixture before churning.

CARAMEL CHOCOLATE ICE CREAM

*Thought by some to be the best ice cream in the world, this special recipe of the Cipriani family,
of the famed Harry's Bar in Venice, was given to me on a visit there.*

MAKES 3 CUPS

4 large egg yolks ▪
2/3 cup sugar, plus 2 tablespoons extra ▪
2 cups whole milk ▪
2/3 cup roughly chopped dark chocolate ▪
1/3 cup unsweetened cocoa powder, ▪
preferably Dutch style

Put the egg yolks in a bowl and beat with a hand whisk or electric beaters until just combined. Gradually add the 2/3 cup sugar and continue beating until the mixture is creamy, pale, and increased in volume, about 3 minutes.

Put the milk in a saucepan and bring to a boil. Remove from the heat and very slowly pour it into the yolk mixture, stirring constantly and quickly to avoid the eggs curdling.

Melt the chocolate in a heatproof bowl over hot water and stir until smooth and satiny. Pour into the custard mixture and stir well to blend. Sift the cocoa powder into the mixture and mix well.

Pour the mixture into a large saucepan and place over medium heat. Do not allow to boil. Stir the mixture until it thickens enough to coat the back of a wooden spoon.

In a small saucepan, heat the 2 tablespoons sugar with 2 teaspoons water to form a dark brown caramel (do not allow to burn). Do not stir; instead, swirl the saucepan.

Add the caramel to the custard and blend thoroughly.

Remove from the heat and pour into a clean bowl. Allow to cool, then refrigerate for 2–4 hours, or until cold. Pour the mixture into an ice-cream machine and churn according to the manufacturer's instructions, then freeze until ready to serve.

VARIATION
Toast 1/3 cup hazelnuts, roughly chop and add to the mixture just before completion of churning.

MILK CHOCOLATE GANACHE ICE CREAM

This delicious and versatile ice cream may be enhanced with other ingredients.

MAKES ABOUT 6 CUPS

CHOCOLATE GANACHE
½ cup whipping cream ▪
1⅓ cups finely chopped milk chocolate ▪

ICE-CREAM BASE
2 cups whole milk ▪
9 oz superfine sugar ▪
5 large egg yolks ▪
1½ cups whipping cream ▪

CHOCOLATE GANACHE
Bring the cream to boiling point in a small saucepan. Remove from the heat, add the chocolate, allow to stand for 1 minute, then stir until smooth.

ICE-CREAM BASE
In a medium saucepan, heat the milk and half the sugar, stirring occasionally, until the sugar is dissolved, and the mixture just comes to a boil.

Using an electric mixer, beat the remaining sugar and the egg yolks in a bowl, then slowly pour the hot milk over the egg mixture, whisking until combined. Return the mixture to the cleaned saucepan and heat gently, stirring with a wooden spoon, until the mixture thickens enough to coat the back of the spoon. Strain immediately into a bowl.

Stir in the cream and Chocolate Ganache. Cover and refrigerate for several hours, or overnight if possible.

Churn in an ice-cream machine according to the manufacturer's instructions; depending on the capacity of your machine, you may need to do this in two batches.

VARIATIONS
Replace the milk chocolate with dark or white chocolate.

CHOCOLATE CHIP
Add ⅔ cup finely chopped dark chocolate 2 minutes before the completion of churning.

HAZELNUT LIQUEUR
Add ½ cup toasted, skinned and finely chopped hazelnuts, plus 1 tablespoon Frangelico liqueur, 2 minutes before the completion of churning.

COFFEE LIQUEUR
Add 1 tablespoon coffee liqueur to the mixture 5 minutes before the completion of churning.

CHOCOLATE MARQUIS

Marquis is a rich, dense mixture similar to a terrine, and is served in slices.
It can be made in one large or two smaller molds.

SERVES 10–12

- 2 cups whole milk
- 6 large egg yolks
- ½ cup superfine sugar
- 1¼ cups unsalted butter, chopped
- 3⅓ cups chopped dark chocolate
- 2 tablespoons chocolate liqueur or coffee liqueur, or freshly brewed espresso coffee

Butter a 5 x 9 inch x 3 inch deep mold, terrine, pyrex loaf pan or bread pan, or a 9 inch springform cake pan, or two 3½ cup terrine molds. Line the mold(s) with plastic wrap, extending the wrap over the sides to allow for easy removal later.

Bring the milk to a boil in a saucepan.

Using an electric mixer, beat the egg yolks and sugar together in a bowl, then gradually beat in the hot milk until just combined.

Place the bowl over a saucepan of simmering water and cook, stirring constantly, for 10–15 minutes, or until the mixture coats the back of a wooden spoon. Strain into a bowl.

Melt the butter and chocolate in a heatproof bowl over hot water. Add to the custard along with the liqueur and mix together. Pour into the prepared mold(s).

Freeze for 2–3 hours, or refrigerate overnight. To serve, cut into slices with a hot dry knife.

VARIATIONS
For a lighter version, 1 cup cream, whipped to soft peaks, may be folded into the chocolate mixture in two additions at the final stage of preparation.

Milk or white chocolate may replace the dark chocolate.

PRALINE VERSION
Make the marquis in two molds—one plain, and the other with 1 cup of Nut Praline (page 112) folded into the mixture.

FOOD OF THE GODS TORTE

The scientific name for the cacao bush, from which chocolate is derived, translates as 'food of the gods'—surely an apt description for this sensational dessert of chocolate, date-and-almond meringue, flavored cream, and berries.

SERVES 8–10

6 large egg whites ■
¾ cup superfine sugar ■
⅔ cup roughly chopped almonds ■
1⅓ cups roughly chopped dark chocolate ■
3½ oz finely sliced pitted dates ■

DECORATION
1¼ cups whipping cream ■
1 tablespoon brandy or whisky (optional), ■
or 2 teaspoons natural vanilla extract
Extra superfine sugar, to taste ■
1⅓ cups fresh blueberries or raspberries ■
⅓ cup shaved dark chocolate ■

Preheat the oven to 315°F. Brush the base and side of a 9–9½ inch springform pan thoroughly with melted butter. Line the base with a round of parchment paper, then butter the paper.

Using an electric mixer, beat the egg whites in a clean, dry bowl until stiff peaks form. Gradually beat in the sugar to form a glossy meringue. Using a rubber spatula, fold in the almonds, chocolate and dates.

Spoon the mixture into the prepared pan. Using a spatula, spread out to the edge of the pan and smooth the top.

Bake for 45 minutes, or until firm to the touch. Cover with foil if the top becomes too brown.

Turn off the heat, open the oven door slightly and allow the meringue to cool in the pan. Remove from the oven, cover the pan loosely and chill overnight. (This ensures easy cutting; the meringue tends to crumble if cut when it is too fresh.)

Release the sides of the pan carefully. Using a spatula, loosen the meringue base from the parchment paper. Slide the meringue onto a serving plate.

DECORATION
Combine the cream, brandy, whisky or vanilla, and superfine sugar, then whip the cream until soft peaks form. Spoon the cream over the meringue and garnish the cake with berries. Decorate with shaved chocolate.

WHITE CHOCOLATE CHEESECAKE

This has become a special-occasion cheesecake in our family.
The creamy rich texture contrasts well with the sharpness of fresh berries.

SERVES 16

PASTRY CRUST
2 cups all-purpose flour ▪
7 oz chilled unsalted butter, chopped ▪
2/3 cup lightly packed light brown sugar ▪
1 cup ground almonds ▪
1 large egg yolk ▪

FILLING
4 cups cream cheese, at room temperature ▪
1 cup superfine sugar ▪
1 teaspoon natural vanilla extract ▪
3½ fl oz milk ▪
3½ cups chopped white chocolate, melted and cooled ▪
5 large eggs, beaten ▪

DECORATION (OPTIONAL)
Strawberries ▪
White chocolate curls or rolls (page 233) ▪

PASTRY CRUST
Using the paddle attachment and large bowl of an electric mixer, or in a food processor, blend together the sifted flour, butter, brown sugar, almonds, and egg yolk until just combined. Bring the ingredients together by hand to form a dough. Wrap in plastic wrap and refrigerate for 30 minutes.

Butter a 10 inch springform cake pan. Roll out the pastry between two sheets of plastic wrap or parchment paper until large enough to fit the pan. Transfer the pastry to the pan, and press it into the base and side. Note that the pastry will be quite soft. Chill for about 2 hours.

Preheat the oven to 315°F.

Cover the pastry with parchment paper and fill with baking weights, rice or dried beans. Bake for 20 minutes. Remove the paper and weights and bake for a further 5–10 minutes, or until pale golden in color. Allow to cool.

FILLING
Using an electric mixer, beat the cream cheese, sugar and vanilla extract until creamy. Add the milk and melted chocolate, and finally fold in the beaten eggs. Beat until smooth. Pour the mixture into the cooked pastry base and bake at 315°F for 50–60 minutes. The filling should still be slightly wobbly in the center; it will continue to cook on standing and will become firmer as it cools. Turn off the heat, open the oven door slightly, and allow the cheesecake to cool in the oven. Chill for 3 hours or overnight before serving. Decorate with strawberries and chocolate curls.

VARIATIONS
PASSIONFRUIT
Add the grated zest of 1 lemon and 1/3 cup strained passionfruit pulp at the same time as the beaten eggs. Decorate with the pulp of 4–6 passionfruit.

RASPBERRY
Sprinkle 2 cups of fresh or frozen raspberries over the cheesecake before baking. Serve with Berry Sauce (page 232) made with raspberries.

CHOCOLATE PANNA COTTA

Make the panna cotta the day before serving. For variation, make a fruit jelly to contrast with the richness of the custard. The jelly layer is set in the molds first, then the chocolate custard layer is added.

SERVES 6

4 fl oz whole milk ▪
14 fl oz whipping cream ▪
½ cup superfine sugar ▪
1 vanilla bean, split ▪
1 cup chopped dark, milk or white chocolate, melted ▪
2½ teaspoons powdered gelatin ▪

Fresh raspberries, almond bread or ▪
Chocolate Brandy Snap Baskets (page 131), to serve

Put the milk, cream, sugar, and the split vanilla bean in a saucepan and gently bring to a simmer. Remove the vanilla bean and, using the tip of a small knife, strip out the seeds, returning them to the mixture (the pod can be washed, dried, and reused). Add the melted chocolate and stir until smooth.

In a small bowl, soften the gelatin in ¼ cup water, then stand the bowl over a saucepan of hot water to dissolve the gelatin. Stir into the hot chocolate cream mixture. Pour the mixture into six 1 cup ramekins, molds or teacups. Refrigerate for 4–6 hours, or overnight. Serve with fresh raspberries and almond bread or brandy snaps.

VARIATIONS

Fill the lower third of the ramekin with one of the following fruit jellies, refrigerate until set, then pour the chocolate custard over the top. Return to the refrigerator to allow the chocolate custard to set.

PASSIONFRUIT JELLY

1½ teaspoons powdered gelatin ▪
Pulp of 3 passionfruit ▪
½ cup freshly squeezed orange juice ▪
⅓ cup superfine sugar ▪

Combine the gelatine with ¼ cup water in a small bowl. Stir to soften, then stand the bowl over a saucepan of hot water to dissolve the gelatin. Strain the passionfruit pulp and orange juice into a small saucepan. Add the sugar and 3½ fl oz water, stir and bring to a boil. Stir the dissolved gelatin into the passionfruit syrup. Allow to cool, then pour into the bottom of the molds.

MANGO JELLY

1½ teaspoons powdered gelatin ▪
1 large ripe mango (about 14 oz), peeled and pulped ▪
Juice of ½ lemon ▪
⅓ cup superfine sugar ▪

Combine the gelatin with ¼ cup water in a small bowl. Stir to soften, then stand the bowl over a saucepan of hot water to dissolve the gelatin. Combine the mango pulp and lemon juice and set aside. In a small saucepan over low heat, combine the sugar and 3½ fl oz water, stirring. Bring to a boil, then remove from the heat. Cool and add to the mango pulp. Stir the dissolved gelatin into the mango pulp. Allow to cool, then pour into the bottom of the molds.

RASPBERRY JELLY

2 teaspoons powdered gelatin ▪
⅓ cup superfine sugar ▪
1 cup fresh or frozen raspberries ▪

Combine the gelatin with ¼ cup water in a small bowl. Stir to soften, then stand the bowl over a saucepan of hot water to dissolve the gelatin. In a small saucepan, combine the sugar and 1 cup water, and bring to a boil. Remove from the heat. Add the raspberries and allow to stand for 2–3 hours. Mash the fruit and strain through a fine strainer, allowing the syrup to drip through, rather than pressing on the solids; this will ensure a clear jelly. Stir the dissolved gelatin into the raspberry syrup. Allow to cool, then pour into the bottom of the molds.

CHOCOLATE DESSERT CUPS

Chocolate cups are a pretty way to present chocolate mousse or ice cream. This is one recipe for which compound chocolate can be used, especially if children will be making the baskets, as it is a little easier to handle than proper chocolate.

MAKES 8

1¾ cups finely chopped white, ■
milk or dark chocolate, melted

To make the cups, you will need wide-based glasses or styrene cups to act as molds, and heavy plastic (a clean, heavy-duty plastic garbage bag will suffice). Cut the plastic into pieces about 8 inches square, depending on the size of the molds you are using.

Place the plastic on a flat surface. Spoon about 1 tablespoon of melted chocolate onto the plastic to a diameter of about 5 inches. Smooth out using a spatula.

Leave the disc for a few moments to firm slightly, then gently place, plastic side down, over the base of an upturned mold set on a small plate. Arrange the plastic to form loose folds around the mold.

Repeat this process until all of the chocolate is used; it is a good idea to make extra cups in case of breakage. Refrigerate the molds for about 10 minutes before unmolding.

To unmold the cups, remove them from the refrigerator, one at a time. Avoid touching the chocolate with your fingers (a tissue held in the hand when working helps prevent chocolate from melting; alternatively, wear cotton gloves).

Gently peel back the plastic from the center of each fold and continue gently peeling until the plastic is removed. Return the cups to the refrigerator for 30 minutes to harden.

Tips
- Store the cups in a covered container.
- Although the cups can be made with chocolate that has simply been melted, chocolate that has been tempered (see page 14) results in a shiny and delicate finish, and the finished product does not require refrigeration.
- These cups can be made up to one week in advance if using tempered chocolate.

CHOCOLATE CRÈME BRÛLÉE

Caramel and chocolate are perfect partners in this classic dessert.

SERVES 8–10

CHOCOLATE CUSTARD CREAM
3 cups whipping cream ▪
1 cup whole milk ▪
½ cup sugar ▪
1¼ cups chopped dark chocolate ▪
1¼ cups chopped milk chocolate ▪
8 egg yolks ▪

CARAMEL TOPPING
½ cup superfine sugar ▪

Preheat the oven to 300°F. Butter an 8 cup shallow ovenproof dish, 1 cup ramekins.

CHOCOLATE CUSTARD CREAM
Put the cream, milk, and sugar in a large saucepan and bring to a boil. Remove from the heat, add the chopped dark and milk chocolates, and allow to stand for 2 minutes, then stir until smooth.

Using an electric mixer, beat the yolks in a bowl, then gradually add the chocolate mixture and beat until combined. Strain the custard into the prepared dish.

Stand the dish or ramekins in a roasting pan and position the pan in the oven. Add enough hot water to the roasting pan to come halfway up the sides of the dish or ramekins.

Bake for 45–60 minutes for the large dish and 25–30 minutes for individual ramekins, or until the custard is set and a knife inserted in the center comes out clean. The custard should still be slightly wobbly in the center; it will continue to cook on standing, and will become firmer as it cools. Carefully remove the dish from the roasting pan. Allow to cool, then refrigerate until required.

CARAMEL TOPPING
Using paper towels, remove the moisture, if any, from the surface of the chilled custard. Sprinkle the surface evenly with the sugar.

Position under a preheated broiler or use a small blow torch to caramelize the sugar. Allow to cool, then refrigerate for at least 4 hours, or preferably overnight. To serve, smash the toffee with the back of a serving spoon.

FLOURLESS HAZELNUT MOUSSE TORTE

This delectable recipe contains a double hit of chocolate, in both the cake and the mousse topping, along with nuts and coffee for good measure.

SERVES 12–16

- 1⅓ cups chopped dark chocolate, melted
- ½ cup freshly brewed espresso coffee
- ¾ cup unsalted butter, at room temperature
- ⅓ cup superfine sugar
- 5 large eggs, separated
- 1 teaspoon natural vanilla extract
- 1⅔ cups ground hazelnuts

- 1 quantity Dark Chocolate Mousse Filling (page 224)

Preheat the oven to 325°F. Butter a 9 inch springform cake pan and line it with parchment paper.

Combine the melted chocolate and hot coffee, stir, and set aside.

Using an electric mixer, cream the butter and sugar until pale and fluffy. Add the egg yolks, one at a time, while continuing to beat.

Using a rubber spatula, fold in the chocolate mixture and vanilla extract, then the ground hazelnuts.

Using clean, dry beaters, beat the egg whites until stiff peaks form, then fold them into the chocolate mixture in two batches.

Pour the mixture into the prepared pan and bake for 45 minutes, or until cooked when tested with a skewer. Allow to cool in the pan.

Spread the mousse onto the cooled cake while it is still in the pan and refrigerate for at least 4 hours, or preferably overnight.

To serve, release the spring on the cake pan and remove the side of the pan. Using a small vegetable knife, ease the paper away from the cake and peel it off.

VARIATION
Ground almonds may replace the hazelnuts.

SUPER CHOCOLATE SORBET

*This recipe is best prepared a day or more before it is needed;
it becomes firmer on the days following the churning.*

MAKES 4 CUPS

½ cup superfine sugar ■
½ cup light corn syrup or liquid glucose ■
⅔ cup chopped dark chocolate ■
¾ cup unsweetened cocoa powder, ■
preferably Dutch style, sifted through a fine sieve

In a saucepan, combine all the ingredients along with 2 cups water, and gently bring to a boil, whisking with a wire whisk. Simmer for 3–5 minutes.

Pour the mixture through a fine sieve into a chilled bowl and leave to cool, then cover and refrigerate for 2–3 hours.

Whisk the chilled sorbet briefly until smooth. Pour the mixture into an ice-cream machine and churn according to the manufacturer's instructions until smooth. Store in the freezer until ready to serve.

CHOCOLATE BRANDY SNAP BASKETS

*Crunchy, caramel-flavored brandy snaps provide a textural contrast to the creaminess of ice cream.
They make a particularly attractive presentation when draped over molds to form baskets.*

MAKES 6

¼ cup unsalted butter ■
¼ cup firmly packed soft brown sugar ■
⅓ cup dark corn syrup or honey ■
½ cup all-purpose flour ■
2 teaspoons ground ginger ■

1⅓ cups chopped dark chocolate, melted, ■
for painting baskets
Ice cream, to serve ■

Preheat the oven to 325°F. Very lightly butter two large or three small baking sheets. Lightly oil heatproof glasses or jars, or the bases of upturned muffin pans, to act as molds.

Melt the butter in a saucepan with the sugar and dark corn syrup or honey over low heat, stirring until all the ingredients are combined. Remove from the heat and cool until lukewarm.

Sift the flour and ginger together. Stir into the butter mixture until smooth. Drop tablespoons of mixture onto the prepared baking sheets, allowing room for spreading. Allow 2 biscuits per sheet. Bake for 8 minutes, or until well spread, bubbling, and golden brown.

Stand for 1–2 minutes until beginning to firm, then remove carefully with a spatula and, using your hands, gently mold the cookie around the base of a prepared mold. Allow to form natural folds. Leave until firm.

When set, remove carefully. Use a pastry brush to paint the inside with the melted and slightly cooled chocolate. Leave to set. To serve, fill the brandy snap baskets with scoops of ice cream.

MILK CHOCOLATE SEMIFREDDO

Semifreddo—Italian for 'half-frozen'—is a delicate and delicious ice cream made without an ice-cream machine.
Dark or white chocolate may replace the milk chocolate.

SERVES 10–12

2 cups whipping cream ■
5 large eggs, separated ■
½ cup superfine sugar ■
2⅔ cups chopped milk chocolate, melted ■
1½ cups hazelnuts, toasted, ■
skinned and chopped (see Note, page 95)
2 tablespoons liqueur, such as Frangelico ■

Line a 9 x 5 x 3 inch loaf or bread pan with plastic wrap, extending the wrap over the edges of the pan to allow for easy removal later.

Whip the cream until soft peaks form, 2–3 minutes. Cover and refrigerate until needed.

Put the egg yolks and half the sugar in a large heatproof bowl over a saucepan of simmering water (ensuring that the base of the bowl does not touch the water) and beat until thick, pale, and increased in volume. Remove from the heat.

Stir in the melted chocolate, chopped hazelnuts, and liqueur. Fold the whipped cream into this mixture.

Using clean beaters, beat the egg whites in a clean, dry bowl on high speed until soft peaks form, 2–3 minutes, then gradually add the remaining sugar. Beat until stiff peaks form. Fold the meringue into the chocolate mixture in two additions.

Pour into the prepared mold. Cover with plastic wrap and freeze overnight. To serve, unmold, remove the plastic wrap, and slice thickly. Serve immediately.

VARIATION
If making a white chocolate version, replace the hazelnuts with toasted blanched almonds, and add about 2 tablespoons orange liqueur for an alternative flavor combination.

WHITE CHOCOLATE MOUSSE

The mousse may be made in individual ramekins or in one large dish.
The latter is an easy and impressive way of serving it for a buffet.

SERVES 6–8

2 cups chopped white chocolate, melted ▪
4 large eggs, separated ▪
1 tablespoon boiling water ▪
2 cups whipping cream ▪
1 tablespoon superfine sugar ▪
2 tablespoons liqueur, such as Cointreau, ▪
Crème de Cacao or Frangelico

Chocolate curls or rolls (page 233), to decorate (optional) ▪

Melt the chocolate gently in a heatproof bowl over hot water, ensuring that the base of the bowl does not touch the water.

In a large bowl of an electric mixer, beat the egg yolks until pale and increased in volume, about 3 minutes, then beat in the warm chocolate. Add the boiling water, beating continuously. Allow to cool.

Using clean beaters, whip the cream until soft peaks form, then fold it into the chocolate mixture using a rubber spatula.

Using clean beaters, beat the egg whites and the sugar in a clean, dry bowl until soft peaks form. Using a rubber spatula, fold this mixture into the chocolate mixture, then fold in the liqueur.

Spoon the mousse into 6–8 individual 1 cup dishes or one 6-cup dish and refrigerate for 24 hours before serving. Alternatively, for a frozen mousse, place the dish(es) in the freezer for at least 4 hours before serving. Remove from the refrigerator 10 minutes before serving.

Decorate with chocolate curls, if desired.

chapter seven

HOT CHOCOLATE

When there's a chill in the air, and our thoughts drift to comfort food,
few things satisfy cold-weather cravings like hot chocolate desserts. Fragrant soufflés,
hearty steamed puddings, delicate crepes, and scrumptious tarts; all provide plenty
of reasons to stay indoors, keep warm, and indulge.

WARM CHOCOLATE MELTING CAKES

These gooey-centered, delicious little steamed puddings are an ideal dessert for a cold winter's evening.

SERVES 6

Superfine sugar, for dusting ▪
1²/₃ cups chopped dark chocolate ▪
1 cup unsalted butter ▪
4 large eggs, separated ▪
½ cup superfine sugar ▪
½ cup all-purpose flour ▪

Berry Sauce (page 232) and heavy cream, crème anglaise, ▪
or French vanilla ice cream, to serve

Preheat the oven to 375°F. Butter six 1 cup ramekins, then dust the insides with sugar, tapping out any excess.

Melt the chocolate and butter together in a bowl over a saucepan of simmering water, making sure that the base of the bowl does not touch the water. Set aside to cool.

Using an electric mixer, beat the egg yolks and sugar on high speed for about 5 minutes, until the mixture is thick and pale, and leaves ribbon-like trails when the beaters are lifted.

Sift the flour over the egg-yolk mixture. Add the melted chocolate mixture and fold in using a rubber spatula.

Using clean, dry beaters, beat the egg whites in a clean, dry bowl until soft peaks form, then fold into the chocolate mixture. Spoon the mixture into the prepared ramekins, then place on a baking sheet.

Bake until the centers start to puff and the tops begin to crack, 12–15 minutes, or until a skewer inserted into the center comes out with thick batter attached. Cool on a wire rack for 10 minutes.

To unmold, run a small sharp knife around the edge of the ramekin. Turn out onto dessert plates and serve with raspberry sauce and heavy cream, crème anglaise, or French vanilla ice cream.

HOT OVEN-BAKED SOUFFLÉ PANCAKES

This recipe was a great favorite when I taught at the Polytech in Regent Street, London, in the fabulous sixties.

SERVES 4

cornstarch, for dusting ▪
8 large egg whites ▪
⅓ cup superfine sugar ▪
4 large egg yolks ▪
⅓ cup all-purpose flour ▪
1 tablespoon unsweetened cocoa powder, ▪
preferably Dutch style
½ cup ground hazelnuts ▪
½ cup grated or finely chopped dark chocolate ▪
Pure confectioner's sugar, sifted ▪

Dark Chocolate Sauce (page 230) and French vanilla ▪
ice cream or whipped cream, to serve

Preheat the oven to 350°F. Butter four ovenproof dessert-sized plates or ovenproof dishes, about 7 inches in diameter, then dust with cornstarch, tapping out any excess.

Using an electric mixer, beat the egg whites in a clean, dry bowl until soft peaks form. Add the superfine sugar and continue beating for 2–3 minutes, or until the sugar is dissolved and a thick, smooth meringue forms.

Fold the egg yolks, sifted flour, and cocoa powder, ground hazelnuts, and chocolate into the meringue until well combined.

Divide the mixture among the prepared plates or dishes, shaping it into a mound. Bake for 10–12 minutes, or until the pancake springs back when lightly touched.

Dust with sifted confectioner's sugar, then slide a spatula under each pancake and fold it in half. Transfer to serving plates and serve at once with hot chocolate sauce and French vanilla ice cream or whipped cream.

Tip
▪ Instead of baking them, the pancakes may be cooked one at a time in a buttered frying pan for 2–3 minutes on top of the stove, and then quickly finished under a hot broiler.

PISTACHIO SOUFFLÉS WITH MILK CHOCOLATE GANACHE CENTERS

SERVES 6

Superfine sugar, for dusting ■

MILK CHOCOLATE GANACHE
½ cup whipping cream ■
1 cup finely chopped milk chocolate ■

SOUFFLÉ
¾ cup whole milk ■
½ cup whipping cream ■
¾ cup unsalted butter ■
½ cup all-purpose flour, sifted ■
⅔ cup finely chopped dark chocolate ■
5 large eggs, separated ■
⅓ cup finely chopped unsalted pistachio nuts ■

Pure confectioner's sugar, for dusting ■

Preheat the oven to 400°F. Butter six 1 cup ramekins, then dust with sugar, tapping out any excess.

MILK CHOCOLATE GANACHE
Bring the cream just to a boil in a small saucepan. Remove from the heat, add the chocolate, allow to stand for 2 minutes, then stir until smooth. Allow the mixture to cool to room temperature, then chill until it can be molded. Form into a log, wrap in plastic wrap, and freeze.

SOUFFLÉ
Warm the milk and cream in a small saucepan until lukewarm.

Melt the butter in a saucepan, remove from the heat and stir in the flour. Gradually add the hot milk mixture, stirring to prevent lumps from forming. Return to a low heat and stir until the sauce is smooth and thick. Remove from the heat. Stir in the chopped chocolate and the beaten egg yolks.

Using an electric mixer, beat the egg whites until soft peaks form. Using a rubber spatula, fold the egg whites gently into the chocolate mixture in two additions. When folding in the second addition of egg white, add the pistachios also.

Spoon a rounded tablespoon of mixture into each ramekin. Slice the ganache log into six equal portions and then gently place a piece of ganache into each ramekin. Spoon in the remaining mixture and smooth the surface.

Bake for 15–20 minutes, until firm on top and well risen. Serve immediately, dusted with sifted confectioner's sugar.

Tips
■ The soufflé base (up to and including the addition of the chocolate and egg yolks) can be made ahead of time. Put the mixture in a bowl and cover with plastic wrap until required. To continue preparation, warm the base mixture gently over hot water and then continue with the addition of the beaten egg whites.
■ The ganache can be made and frozen the day before the soufflés are made.

CHOCOLATE RUM SELF-SAUCING PUDDING

I developed this recipe for my friend Dur-é Dara to use in her restaurant, where it has been a great hit.
The pudding should be strongly flavored with rum and dark with chocolate, so buy only the best for this dessert.

SERVES 6

Preheat the oven to 350°F. Butter six 1 cup soufflé dishes or a 4 cup pie dish.

⅓ cup unsalted butter ▪
⅔ cup chopped dark chocolate ▪
1 large egg ▪
½ cup superfine sugar ▪
1 cup all-purpose flour ▪
2 teaspoons baking powder ▪
2 tablespoons Dutch-style or French Valrhona ▪
cocoa powder, sifted
½ cup milk ▪

Melt the butter in a saucepan over low heat, add the chocolate, and stir until melted. Set aside to cool.

Whisk the egg and caster sugar together in a small bowl until pale and creamy, then add to the melted chocolate.

Sift the flour, baking powder, and cocoa powder together. Add to the mixture in two batches along with the milk. Beat the batter with a wooden spoon until smooth. Spoon the mixture into the prepared dish(es) and place on an oven sheet.

SAUCE
½ cup lightly packed soft brown sugar ▪
2 tablespoons Dutch-style or French Valrhona cocoa powder ▪
1½ cups boiling water ▪
2–3 tablespoons dark rum, orange liqueur, or coffee liqueur ▪

Heavy cream or vanilla ice cream, to serve ▪

SAUCE
Sift the brown sugar and cocoa powder together, and sprinkle evenly over the top of each pudding.

Combine the boiling water and rum or liqueur and pour evenly and carefully over the cake mix. Bake for 15–20 minutes for individual puddings, or 40 minutes for one large pudding, or until puffed and firm to the touch.

If making individual puddings, turn them out while still hot into shallow dessert bowls. Serve the large pudding straight from the pie dish. Serve with heavy cream or vanilla ice cream.

VARIATIONS
Any of the following additions can be folded into the mixture after it has been beaten with the wooden spoon:

⅓ cup toasted, peeled, and chopped hazelnuts with ¼ cup chocolate chips and 3 tablespoons raisins, cut in half and soaked in brandy for 1–2 hours or overnight

⅓ cup chopped pitted dates

⅓ cup pitted and halved cherries, soaked in orange liqueur for 2 hours.

CREPES WITH CHOCOLATE COCONUT SAUCE

The batter for this dessert, or the crepes themselves, can be prepared ahead of time.
The crepes are particularly delicious when served with seasonal fruits.

SERVES 6–8

CREPES
1 cup all-purpose flour ■
1 tablespoon superfine sugar ■
2 large eggs ■
2 large egg yolks ■
1¼ cups milk ■
1 tablespoon unsalted butter, melted ■
2 tablespoons chocolate liqueur (optional) ■
Extra butter, for cooking ■

NUT FILLING
1 cup whipping cream ■
½ cup chopped unsalted macadamia nuts ■
1 tablespoon pure confectioner's sugar ■

CHOCOLATE COCONUT SAUCE
⅔ cup chopped dark chocolate ■
½ cup whipping cream ■
¼ cup grated dried coconut ■

Fresh berries, to serve (optional) ■
Mint, to garnish (optional) ■

CREPES
Sift the flour and sugar into a bowl.

In another bowl, whisk together the eggs and egg yolks until pale and creamy. Add the milk, melted butter, and liqueur, if using.

Make a well in the center of the flour and pour in the liquid. Beat with a wooden spoon until the mixture is smooth. Cover and allow to stand for 1 hour.

Cook the crepes one at a time in a lightly buttered crepe pan. Keep the cooked crepes warm while you cook the rest of the batter.

NUT FILLING
Whip the cream, add the macadamia nuts and confectioner's sugar, and fold in gently.

Divide the filling evenly and spread over half of each crepe. Fold the crepes and place on a serving plate.

CHOCOLATE COCONUT SAUCE
Combine all ingredients in a small saucepan and stir over low heat until the chocolate has melted. Pour the sauce over the crepes.

If desired, serve with fresh berries and garnish with mint.

Tip
■ The crepes can be prepared in advance; stack them with parchment paper in between, cover, and refrigerate. To warm, place the crepes on a baking sheet lined with parchment paper, cover with another piece of baking paper, and heat in a preheated 350°F oven for about 5 minutes.

STICKY DATE PUDDING CAKE

Winter comfort food par excellence! Any leftovers can be rewarmed in the microwave oven in 20-second intervals until heated through, or covered with foil and reheated in a moderate oven for 5 minutes or so.

SERVES 9

CAKE
1½ cups chopped pitted dates ▪
1 teaspoon baking soda ▪
½ cup unsalted butter, at room temperature ▪
⅔ cup superfine sugar ▪
2 large eggs, lightly beaten ▪
1½ cup) self-rising flour ▪
1 cup chopped dark chocolate, melted and cooled ▪

CARAMEL SAUCE
½ cup unsalted butter ▪
⅔ cup lightly packed soft brown sugar ▪
1 cup whipping cream ▪
1 teaspoon natural vanilla extract ▪

Whipped cream, to serve ▪

Preheat the oven to 350°F. Butter a deep 8 inch square cake pan, then line the base with parchment paper.

CAKE
Put the dates in a saucepan, cover with 1 cup water, bring to a boil and simmer for 3 minutes. Add the baking soda. Set aside to cool slightly.

Using an electric mixer, beat the butter and sugar until pale and fluffy. Add the eggs gradually, beating well after each addition.

Fold in the sifted flour, then the date mixture. Stir well until combined, then fold in the cooled melted chocolate.

Pour the mixture into the prepared pan. Bake for 40–45 minutes, or until the cake shrinks back from the sides of the pan.

CARAMEL SAUCE
Make the sauce while the cake is baking. Combine the butter, sugar, and cream in a saucepan and bring to a boil, stirring. Reduce the heat and simmer for 5 minutes. Remove from the heat and add the vanilla extract.

To serve, cut the warm cake into nine squares and place on warm plates. Pour the hot sauce over and serve with whipped cream.

FLOURLESS CHOCOLATE SOUFFLÉ

Soufflés have an undeservedly intimidating reputation, but they are really not difficult to prepare.
The base mixture and ramekins can be prepared in advance, with the egg whites beaten and added just before baking.

SERVES 8

Superfine sugar, for dusting ■

1⅓ cups chopped dark chocolate ■
3 tablespoons strong freshly brewed coffee ■
½ cup unsalted butter, at room temperature ■
8 large eggs, separated ■
4 large egg whites ■
Pinch of cream of tartar ■
¼ cup superfine sugar ■

Whipped cream or Dark Chocolate Sauce (page 230), to serve ■

Preheat the oven to 400°F. Butter eight ¾ cup ramekins, then dust the insides with superfine sugar, tapping out the excess. Put the ramekins on a baking sheet.

Combine the chocolate, coffee, and butter in a heatproof bowl. Place the bowl over a saucepan of hot water and allow the chocolate to melt, stirring occasionally. Stir until smooth. Remove from the heat and allow to cool to room temperature. Stir in the egg yolks.

Using an electric mixer, beat the egg whites with the cream of tartar until very soft peaks form. Add the sugar gradually and continue to beat until soft peaks form.

Stir one-quarter of the egg whites into the base mixture using a rubber spatula. Fold in the remaining egg whites.

Pour the mixture into the prepared ramekins, filling them to the top. Bake for 15–18 minutes, or until the soufflés are well risen and baked through, except for the very center, which should remain soft and liquid.

Place the ramekins on dessert plates and serve immediately with whipped cream or chocolate sauce, if desired.

Tip
■ Check one soufflé by taking the point of a spoon and using it to lift the top off to one side. The center of the soufflé should look fluffy. Allow the top of the soufflé to fall back into place.

MILK CHOCOLATE FONDUE

Fondues are an ideal way to get children involved at parties. If you don't have a fondue pot,
use a heatproof bowl over a saucepan of simmering water.

SERVES 4–6

1²/₃ cups chopped or grated milk ∎
or dark chocolate
¹/₂ cup whipping cream ∎
2 tablespoons orange juice, or a few drops peppermint or ∎
natural vanilla extract
Marshmallows and/or cookies ∎
Fresh fruit, cut into bite-sized pieces ∎

Put the chocolate and cream in a fondue pot. Heat gently, stirring well, until the chocolate is melted. Add the orange juice or other flavoring and stir to blend.

Secure the food to be dipped on the end of a fondue fork or skewer and dip into the chocolate mixture. Allow to cool a little before eating.

OLD-FASHIONED HOT CHOCOLATE

Traditional French-style hot chocolate contains exactly that—melted chocolate, not just cocoa powder.
Use the best-quality chocolate for a truly decadent winter pick-me-up.

SERVES 4

¹/₂ cup unsweetened cocoa powder, ∎
preferably Dutch style, or good-quality drinking chocolate
¹/₂ cup boiling water ∎
4 cups milk ∎
²/₃ cup chopped dark chocolate ∎
Sugar, to taste ∎
¹/₂ teaspoon natural vanilla extract (optional) ∎

Mini marshmallows and whipped cream, to serve (optional) ∎

Blend the cocoa powder and boiling water to form a paste.

Put the milk and chocolate in a saucepan over medium–low heat. Stir until the chocolate melts.

Pour the hot milk over the cocoa mixture and stir until blended. If using cocoa, sweeten to taste. Add the vanilla. If desired, float mini marshmallows on top and garnish with a swirl of whipped cream.

VARIATION
Substitute milk chocolate for the dark chocolate.

CHOCOLATE TART

A rich, spectacular, warm chocolate dessert tart that may be dressed up, if desired, with a garnish of gold leaf (see page 235) on each serving portion. Serve with heavy cream.

SERVES 6–8

½ quantity Sweet Pie Pastry (page 32) ∎

CHOCOLATE FILLING
7 fl oz whipping cream ∎
1⅓ cups finely chopped dark or milk chocolate ∎
1 teaspoon natural vanilla extract or brandy ∎
2 egg yolks ∎

Heavy cream, to serve ∎

Preheat the oven to 325°F.

Roll out the pastry between two sheets of parchment paper about ¼ inch thick and use it to line four 3¼ inch loose-based tart pans. Note that the pastry is very soft and may crack in places; if it does, patch it with scraps of pastry. Refrigerate for 30 minutes, then trim the edge of the pastry.

Line with crumpled parchment paper, weight with a layer of dried beans or rice and bake blind for 10 minutes.

Remove the paper and beans or rice and bake for 5 minutes more, or until pale golden. Allow to cool.

Reduce the oven temperature to 315°F.

CHOCOLATE FILLING
Bring the cream just to a boil in a small saucepan. Remove from the heat. Add the chopped chocolate, allow to stand for 1 minute, then stir until smooth. Allow to cool to room temperature, then whisk in the vanilla extract or brandy, and the egg yolks.

Spoon the filling into the tart shells. Bake for 25–30 minutes, or until just set. Allow to cool in the pans for 10–15 minutes, then remove the outside of the pans, and cool on a wire rack.

Serve warm or cold with heavy cream.

NOTE To make a 11¼ inch tart, double the quantity of chocolate filling and use 1 quantity of Sweet Shortcrust Pastry.

VARIATION
The quantity given will also make 20–24 tartlets. Fill the pre-baked tartlet shells three-quarters full with chocolate filling, and bake for about 10 minutes, or until just set.

Alternatively, make the recipe as one 7½ inch tart and bake for about 15 minutes, or until just set.

chapter eight

CHOCOLATE INDULGENCE

When a truly wicked and enticing dessert is called for, it's hard to go past chocolate.

Heady liqueur-soaked cakes, dense mousse cakes and mud cakes,

nutty meringue confections, and luscious layered tortes—chocolate offers

many memorable ways to finish a special meal.

CHOCOLATE-GLAZED LEMON CURD CAKE

The cake and curd are both best made the day before they are required, and the cake assembled on the day of serving. The lemon curd contrasts in flavor and color with the rich chocolate glaze. Passionfruit curd could replace the lemon.

SERVES 12–14

LEMON CURD
8 large egg yolks ■
1³/4 cups sugar ■
1¹/2 tablespoons grated lemon zest ■
¹/2 cup lemon juice ■
²/3 cup unsalted butter, chopped ■

CAKE
1²/3 cups blanched almonds, toasted ■
1²/3 cups superfine sugar ■
1¹/3 cups unsalted butter, at room temperature ■
1¹/2 tablespoons grated lemon zest ■
6 large eggs, lightly beaten ■
¹/3 cup lemon juice ■
1¹/2 cups self-rising flour ■

CHOCOLATE GLAZE
3¹/2 fl oz whipping cream ■
1¹/3 cups finely chopped dark chocolate ■

Preheat the oven to 325°F. Butter a 10 inch springform pan and line the base with parchment paper.

LEMON CURD
Whisk the egg yolks just until combined. Place the egg yolks, sugar, zest, and juice in a saucepan. Cook over very low heat, stirring with a wooden spoon, until the mixture thickens and the sugar has dissolved. Do not overheat the mixture, or the eggs will curdle.

Add the butter and continue stirring over low heat until the mixture coats the back of the wooden spoon, about 5 minutes. Pour into a bowl, cover and refrigerate until set (preferably overnight).

CAKE
Grind the almonds and sugar in a food processor until the mixture resembles coarse breadcrumbs. Add the butter and lemon zest and mix well until creamy. Add the eggs gradually. Transfer the mixture to a bowl and fold in the lemon juice and sifted flour.

Pour the mixture into the prepared pan. Bake for 40–50 minutes, or until cooked when tested with a skewer. Allow to cool in the pan.

CHOCOLATE GLAZE
Put the cream in a small saucepan and bring just to a boil. Remove from the heat, add the chocolate, and stir until smooth. Allow to cool until slightly thickened.

To assemble, slice the cake in half horizontally. Place one layer onto a serving plate. Spread with lemon curd to within ¹/2 inch of the edge. Gently place the other cake half on top of the curd layer. Pour the chocolate glaze over the top and allow to set.

Tip
■ The cake may be stored in the refrigerator in an airtight container during hot weather.

ALMOND DACQUOISE WITH CHOCOLATE BUTTERCREAM

With rounds of crunchy meringue nestled between layers of velvety buttercream, this dessert cake is perfect for a special occasion. Ground hazelnuts may replace the almonds. The meringue discs may be made up to a week ahead.

SERVES 10–12

MERINGUE LAYERS
Cornstarch, for dusting ■
1²⁄₃ cups almonds ■
6 large egg whites ■
9 oz superfine sugar ■
1 tablespoon instant coffee granules ■

CHOCOLATE BUTTERCREAM
9 oz sugar ■
6 large egg yolks ■
1 tablespoon freshly brewed strong black coffee ■
1 cup unsalted butter, cubed, at room temperature ■
1¹⁄₃ cups chopped milk or dark chocolate, ■
melted and cooled to tepid

Preheat the oven to 350°F. You will need four large baking sheets lined with parchment paper. Draw a 8 inch circle on each sheet of paper. Butter the paper and dust with sifted cornstarch.

MERINGUE LAYERS
Put the almonds on an oven sheet and toast for 8–10 minutes, stirring occasionally, until golden brown. Allow to cool completely, then process in a food processor until finely ground.

Using an electric mixer, beat the egg whites until stiff peaks form, then gradually beat in the sugar, 2 tablespoons at a time. Continue beating for 2–3 minutes, or until stiff and glossy. Add the sifted coffee granules and ground almonds, and fold them into the egg-white mixture.

Divide the mixture evenly among the four parchment paper circles and spread out to the edges using a spatula. Bake for 25–30 minutes, or until crisp and lightly colored. Allow to cool on the sheets on a wire rack, then peel off the paper.

CHOCOLATE BUTTERCREAM
Mix 1¹⁄₄ cups water and the sugar in a small, heavy-based saucepan. Stir over low heat to dissolve the sugar, then increase the heat and bring to a boil. Boil the mixture for about 6 minutes, or until it reaches 240°F (soft-ball stage) on a sugar thermometer.

Using an electric mixer, beat the egg yolks in a large bowl until combined. Slowly and carefully pour the hot sugar syrup onto the egg yolks while beating continuously. (To prevent spatters, avoid pouring the syrup onto the beaters.) Beat on high speed until thick and creamy, about 5 minutes. Mix in the coffee, then beat in the cubed butter, one piece at a time. Beat the cooled chocolate into the buttercream until thoroughly mixed. Allow the mixture to cool for about 1 hour, or until thickened to a spreadable consistency.

To assemble, sandwich the meringues together using half of the buttercream. Spread the remaining buttercream over the top and side of the cake. Refrigerate for 4 hours or overnight before serving.

Store in an airtight container in the refrigerator for up to 3 days.

BACIO SEMIFREDDO

Delicate layers of crunchy hazelnut and milk chocolate form this impressive speciality cake.
It can be prepared up to a week in advance.

SERVES 12

1 quantity Chocolate Genoise Sponge (page 31), ▪
baked in two 8 inch round cake pans

LIQUEUR SYRUP
3 tablespoons superfine sugar ▪
3 tablespoons liqueur, such as Frangelico, Kirsch, ▪
Cointreau, or brandy

CHOCOLATE HAZELNUT CREAM
1½ teaspoons powdered gelatin ▪
2⅓ cups whipping cream ▪
1 tablespoon superfine sugar ▪
1¼ cups hazelnuts, toasted, skins removed, ▪
processed until finely crushed; or use ground hazelnuts
1 cup chopped milk chocolate, melted ▪

½ quantity Ganache Glaze for Chilled Cakes (page 229) ▪

LIQUEUR SYRUP
Combine ⅓ cup water and the sugar in a small saucepan. Bring the mixture just to a boil and continue to boil, stirring occasionally, until the sugar is dissolved. Allow to cool. Stir in the liqueur. Refrigerate until needed.

CHOCOLATE HAZELNUT CREAM
In a small heatproof bowl, combine the gelatin and 1 tablespoon warm water, allowing the gelatin to soften. Then place the bowl over hot water or in the microwave oven and heat gently until the gelatin is dissolved. Allow to cool.

Beat the cream and sugar together until thickened. Stir in the dissolved gelatin and beat the mixture until soft peaks form.

Fold the hazelnuts into the melted chocolate and fold this mixture into the cream.

To assemble, brush each cake generously with the liqueur syrup. Spread one-third of the hazelnut cream on top of one cake layer. Place the other cake layer on top and spread with another one-third of the hazelnut cream. Coat the top and side of the cake with the remaining hazelnut cream.

Wrap the cake in plastic wrap then foil. Freeze the cake for at least 4–6 hours, or up to a week in advance of serving.

Frost the cake while still frozen with the Ganache Glaze for Chilled Cakes. Allow to sit at room temperature for 30 minutes, then serve.

FLOURLESS ESPRESSO CHOCOLATE CAKE

This cake is my family's favorite. I serve it with heavy cream and fresh raspberries in season.
It is best made the day before it is to be served.

SERVES 8–10

2½ cups chopped dark chocolate ▪
3 tablespoons strong freshly brewed espresso coffee ▪
3 tablespoons coffee liqueur or brandy ▪
4 large eggs ▪
½ cup white sugar ▪
¾ cup whipping cream ▪
¼ cup superfine sugar ▪
1 teaspoon natural vanilla extract ▪

Pure confectioner's sugar, for dusting ▪
Fresh raspberries, to serve ▪
Heavy cream, to serve ▪

Preheat the oven to 350°F. Butter a 8 inch cake pan, line with parchment paper, then butter the paper.

Melt the chocolate with the coffee and liqueur or brandy in a heatproof bowl over hot water. Stir until smooth.

Using an electric mixer, beat the eggs and the white sugar in a heatproof bowl over a saucepan of simmering water for about 10 minutes, or until thickened and almost tripled in volume.

Whip the cream, superfine sugar and vanilla extract until soft peaks form.

Gently fold the chocolate mixture into the egg mixture, then gently fold in the whipped cream.

Pour the mixture into the prepared pan and immediately put the pan in a roasting pan. Pour enough hot water into the roasting pan to reach halfway up the side of the cake pan.

Bake for 50–60 minutes, or until a skewer inserted into the center of the cake comes out almost clean (the skewer will still be slightly moist; the cake will continue to cook as it cools).

Remove from the oven and allow to cool in the pan in the water bath. When cool, do not remove from the pan; cover and refrigerate until ready to serve.

To serve, immerse the cake pan in a little hot water to loosen. Invert onto a wire rack, remove the paper, then invert again onto a serving plate. Dust with confectioner's sugar. Serve with fresh raspberries and heavy cream.

Tip
▪ Cut with a hot, dry, sharp knife.

DOUBLE FUDGE MOUSSE CAKE

The cake and mousse components for this heavenly dessert are quite similar. The cooked cake collapses as it cools, giving a rustic appearance. The center is then filled with the mousse.

SERVES 10

CAKE
2/3 cup unsalted butter ▪
1 cup chopped dark chocolate ▪
5 large eggs, separated ▪
1 tablespoon unsweetened cocoa powder, ▪
preferably Dutch style
3/4 cup superfine sugar ▪

MOUSSE
1/3 cup unsalted butter ▪
2/3 cup chopped dark chocolate ▪
3 large eggs, separated ▪
2 teaspoons unsweetened cocoa powder, ▪
preferably Dutch style
1/2 cup superfine sugar ▪
1 tablespoon coffee liqueur ▪
2 teaspoons powdered gelatin dissolved in ▪
1/3 cup warm water

DECORATION
Chocolate curls or rolls (page 233), to decorate ▪

Preheat the oven to 350°F. Butter a 8–9 inch springform cake pan and line it with parchment paper.

CAKE
Put the butter and chocolate in a heatproof bowl over a saucepan of hot water and allow to stand until melted. Stir until smooth.

Mix the egg yolks with the sifted cocoa powder and stir into the chocolate mixture.

Using an electric mixer, beat the egg whites on high speed until stiff. Gradually add the sugar, beating until it is dissolved after each addition, then continue beating until the mixture is stiff and glossy, 2–3 minutes.

Fold the beaten egg whites into the chocolate mixture in two additions. Pour into the prepared pan and bake for 25–30 minutes. Allow to cool in the pan. Leave the cake in the pan to form a mold for the mousse topping.

MOUSSE
Put the butter and chocolate in a heatproof bowl over a saucepan of hot water and allow to stand until melted. Stir until smooth.

Mix the egg yolks with the sifted cocoa powder and stir into the chocolate mixture.

Using an electric mixer, beat the egg whites on high speed until stiff. Gradually add the sugar, beating until it is dissolved after each addition, then continue beating until the mixture is stiff and glossy, 2–3 minutes.

Fold the beaten egg whites into the chocolate mixture in two additions, along with the liqueur and gelatin. Pour the chocolate mousse carefully over the center of the cooled cake. Cover and refrigerate until set, 3–4 hours or overnight, before unmolding.

VARIATION
3/4 cup finely chopped pecans may be folded into the cake mixture before the egg whites.

TIRAMISÙ CAKE

Tiramisù, the Italian version of trifle, is thought to have originated early in the 18th century in Sienna.
The name means 'pick-me-up', and what could be more reviving than a slice of this delicious dessert cake?

SERVES 12

CAKE
2¼ cups mascarpone cheese ■
½ cup cream cheese ■
2 tablespoons pure confectioner's sugar ■
¼ cup orange liqueur or brandy, ■
plus 2 tablespoons extra
2 teaspoons grated orange zest ■
1¼ cups freshly brewed strong black coffee ■
12 oz lady finger ■

ZABAGLIONE
4 large egg yolks ■
¼ cup superfine sugar ■
½ cup dry white wine ■
3 tablespoons orange liqueur or brandy ■
1 tablespoon lemon juice ■
²/₃ cup chopped dark chocolate, ■
melted and cooled to tepid
½ cup grated dark chocolate, to decorate ■

Butter a 10 inch springform cake pan and line the base and side with foil. Butter the foil.

CAKE
Using an electric mixer, lightly beat together the mascarpone, cream cheese, sifted confectioner's sugar, liqueur or brandy, and orange zest.

Combine the coffee and the extra 2 tablespoons liqueur or brandy in a shallow dish. Dip half of the lady's fingers for 1–2 seconds each into the coffee mixture and arrange them in a layer in the base of the prepared springform pan.

ZABAGLIONE
Using an electric mixer, beat the egg yolks and sugar together in a heatproof bowl until just combined. Place the bowl over a saucepan of simmering water. Gradually beat in the wine, liqueur or brandy, and lemon juice. Beat constantly for 8–10 minutes, or until thick and creamy.

To assemble, combine half the mascarpone mixture with half the zabaglione. Fold gently to combine and pour the mixture over the layer of sponge fingers in the pan.

Dip the remaining sponge fingers in the coffee mixture and arrange them in a layer over the top of the mascarpone mixture. Gently spread the remaining mascarpone mixture over this layer.

Stir the tepid melted chocolate into the remaining zabaglione and gently pour over the surface of the cake.

Refrigerate for at least 10 hours. Just before serving, sprinkle with the grated chocolate, unmold, remove the foil and slice.

CHOCOLATE RICOTTA CHEESECAKE

*Italian-style cheesecakes, such as this one, contain ricotta cheese, which gives a lighter result
than the cream cheese used for American-style cheesecakes. The cake should be made the day before it is to be served.*

SERVES 8–10

FILLING
2⅓ cups ricotta cheese ▪
¾ cup superfine sugar ▪
3 large eggs ▪
¾ cup whipping cream ▪
¾ cup chopped dark, milk or white chocolate, ▪
melted and cooled to tepid
2 tablespoons all-purpose flour ▪
1 teaspoon natural vanilla extract ▪

PASTRY
⅓ cup unsalted butter ▪
¼ cup superfine sugar ▪
1 large egg, beaten ▪
1½ cups all-purpose flour ▪

Butter a 9 inch springform pan.

FILLING
Combine the ricotta cheese, sugar, and eggs in the bowl of a food processor or an electric mixer and blend until smooth. Add the cream, melted chocolate, flour, and vanilla and beat or process until combined.

PASTRY
Using an electric mixer or a food processor, cream the butter and sugar until pale and fluffy. Add the beaten egg, then the sifted flour, and beat until just combined.

Turn the dough out onto a lightly floured work surface and bring together into a ball. Wrap in plastic wrap and allow to rest in the refrigerator for 1 hour. Remove from the refrigerator and leave for about 5 minutes to return to room temperature.

Preheat the oven to 350°F.

Roll out two-thirds of the pastry into a circle and use it to line the base of the pan, letting it come 2 inches up the sides. The pastry is very soft and may break when eased into the pan; if this happens, push the cracks together with your fingers, and patch with some of the remaining pastry if necessary. Pour or spoon the filling into the pastry base.

Roll out the remaining pastry into a rectangle. Using a sharp knife or a fluted pastry wheel, cut the pastry into eight strips about ¾ inch wide. Arrange these in a lattice design (see Tip, below) over the top of the cheesecake. Bake for 1–1¼ hours, or until firm and cooked when tested with a skewer. Allow to cool in the pan on a wire rack. Chill overnight before serving.

Tip
▪ On a piece of parchment paper, draw a circle the diameter of the springform pan. Interlace the lattice strips on the baking paper, trimming to the size of the circle, and place in the freezer to set. Then arrange them on top of the cheesecake before baking, neatly trimming off any excess.

CHOCOLATE TORTE

A beautiful special-occasion cake that can be simply dusted with confectioner's sugar,
or decorated with seasonal berries.

SERVES 10–12

3 cups chopped dark chocolate ■
½ cup brandy, or berry or coffee liqueur ■
¼ cup unsweetened cocoa powder, ■
preferably Dutch style, sifted
1 cup unsalted butter, cut into cubes ■
¾ cup superfine sugar ■
10 large eggs, separated ■
½ cup all-purpose flour ■
¼ teaspoon cream of tartar ■

Pure confectioner's sugar and fresh berries, to serve ■

Preheat the oven to 315°F. Line a 10 inch cake pan with a double layer of foil, then butter the foil.

Heat the chocolate, the brandy or liqueur, ½ cup water, the cocoa, butter, and ½ cup of the sugar in a heatproof bowl over a saucepan of hot water. Using a wooden spoon, stir until smooth. Remove from the heat and allow to cool.

Using an electric mixer, whisk the egg yolks until pale and increased in volume and thick ribbons form when the beaters are lifted from the mixture. Stir the egg yolks into the chocolate mixture. Sift in the flour and, using a rubber spatula, fold in until combined.

Beat the egg whites with the cream of tartar until stiff peaks form. Gradually beat in the remaining sugar. Fold this mixture into the chocolate mixture in two batches. Pour into the prepared pan.

Place the cake pan into a roasting pan and gently pour in enough hot water to come halfway up the side of the cake pan. Bake for 1¼–1½ hours, or until cooked when tested with a skewer.

Remove from the oven and allow to cool completely in the pan before turning out. The cake will shrink a little as it cools. Allow to stand overnight before serving, to allow the flavors to mellow.

To serve, dust with confectioner's sugar and decorate with fresh seasonal berries.

DARK CHOCOLATE MUD CAKE

*Moist, dense, and fragrant with rum or whisky,
mud cake is a modern classic.*

SERVES 8–10

1 cup unsalted butter ▪
2 cups firmly packed soft brown sugar ▪
½ cup hot water ▪
¼ cup whisky or dark rum ▪
1⅔ cups chopped dark chocolate ▪
2 large eggs, beaten ▪
1 teaspoon natural vanilla extract ▪
2 cups all-purpose flour ▪
1 teaspoon baking powder ▪
¼ cup unsweetened cocoa powder, ▪
preferably Dutch style

Pure confectioner's sugar, to dust ▪
Thick cream or vanilla ice cream, to serve ▪

Preheat the oven to 315°F. Butter a 9 inch cake pan and line it with parchment paper.

Melt the butter in a saucepan. Add the sugar, hot water, and whisky or rum and bring to a boil, stirring. Remove from the heat, add the chocolate, and stir with a wooden spoon until the chocolate is melted and the mixture is smooth.

While continuing to beat, gradually add the eggs and vanilla extract. Beat until well mixed. Allow to cool to room temperature.

Sift the flour, baking powder, and cocoa together and gradually fold into the chocolate mixture. Pour into the prepared pan and bake for 60–70 minutes. Test with a skewer; note that as this is a very moist cake, the skewer will not come out completely clean.

Allow to cool completely in the pan on a wire rack before turning out. Dust with confectioner's sugar and serve with thick cream or ice cream.

PANETTONE FARCITO (STUFFED PANETTONE)

Panettone, an Italian speciality, is traditionally made in a cylindrical cake pan, giving a dome-shaped top meant to symbolize the cupolas of Lombardy's churches. This rich, delicious cake improves after one to two days' refrigeration.

SERVES 10–12

1 large panettone, about 2 lb ▪

ZABAGLIONE
4 egg yolks ▪
½ cup superfine sugar ▪
⅔ cup Marsala ▪
2 cups whipping cream ▪
1 cup chopped dark chocolate, melted and cooled to tepid ▪
2 tablespoons Marsala and 1 tablespoon brandy, combined ▪

Peel the paper off the sides and base of the panettone. Horizontally cut the domed top from the panettone. Set aside.

Cut downwards right through the panettone in a cylindrical shape, leaving a ring around the outside about ½ inch thick. Carefully remove the cylindrical center and cut it horizontally into six slices.

ZABAGLIONE
Beat the egg yolks and sugar together in a small saucepan. Gradually add the Marsala, a tablespoon at a time, stirring over low heat, until the mixture is thick and creamy. Pour into a cold bowl and set aside until cool.

Whip the cream in a large bowl until stiff peaks form. Fold the whipped cream into the cooled custard. Transfer half of this mixture to another bowl. Add the cooled melted chocolate to one bowl of custard and fold in until combined.

Broil the panettone slices until they are a light golden color.

To assemble, place the outer ring of the panettone on a serving plate. Replace the base slice of the cylindrical center piece into the bottom of the ring and brush generously with the Marsala and brandy mix. Spread with about one-third of the plain zabaglione. Place another slice of panettone on top, brush with the liqueur mixture and then spread one-third of the chocolate mixture over the panettone. Continue layering the plain zabaglione and then the chocolate zabaglione alternately on slices of panettone until completed, keeping the 'dome' of the panettone as the final layer.

Cover and chill for at least 3–4 hours, or until set and firm.

CHOCOLATE GUGELHOPF

Gugelhopf, a yeast cake traditionally served with afternoon coffee, is baked in a special high fluted cake pan with a central chimney that distributes heat evenly. It may be served dusted with confectioner's sugar or with a delicious chocolate glaze.

SERVES 12

CAKE
4 cups all-purpose flour ▪
½ teaspoon salt ▪
¼ cup superfine sugar ▪
1 tablespoon dry yeast ▪
2 large eggs, beaten ▪
⅓ cup unsalted butter, melted and cooled to tepid ▪
1¼ cups milk, heated to lukewarm ▪
14 oz dark chocolate, melted and cooled ▪

CHOCOLATE GLAZE
2⅔ cups chopped dark chocolate, melted and cooled to tepid ▪
2 tablespoons unsalted butter, at room temperature ▪
1 tablespoon light corn syrup (optional) ▪

Preheat the oven to 400°F. Butter a 10 cup capacity gugelhopf mold or ring pan.

CAKE
Sift the flour and salt into a large bowl. Stir in the sugar and yeast. Add the beaten egg, melted butter and warm milk. Mix well, then turn out onto a floured surface and knead for about 5 minutes, or until a soft dough forms.

Return the dough to the bowl, cover with a clean dish towel and leave in a warm, draught-free place for 30–60 minutes, until it doubles in size.

Turn the dough out again and knead for 5 minutes. Roll out to a 12 x 16 inch rectangle about ½ inch thick. Spread with the melted chocolate. Roll lengthwise, as though making a jelly roll, and place in the buttered gugelhopf mold.

Cover and leave in a warm place to rise again (about 30 minutes).

Bake for about 30 minutes, or until the cake is a light golden color and sounds hollow when tapped.

Cool in the mold for 10 minutes before turning out onto a wire rack. Invert right side up and allow to cool thoroughly.

CHOCOLATE GLAZE
To make the chocolate glaze, beat all the ingredients together and pour over the cold cake.

VARIATIONS
Add 1⅔ cups raisins soaked in 2 tablespoons dark rum along with the beaten egg, melted butter, and warm milk.

Add ⅔ cup chopped blanched almonds with the dark chocolate filling.

QUEEN OF SHEBA CAKE

*Sublime and extremely rich, this cake combines chocolate, orange, and hazelnuts,
and is filled and coated with chocolate ganache.*

SERVES 12–20

Preheat the oven to 325° F. Butter two 10 inch cake pans and line them with parchment paper.

CAKE
- 1½ cups unsalted butter, at room temperature
- 1⅔ cups superfine sugar
- Grated zest of 3 oranges
- 9 large eggs
- 2¼ cups ground hazelnuts
- 2 cups ground almonds
- 2 cups chopped dark chocolate, melted and cooled to tepid

GANACHE FILLING AND FROSTING
- 1½ cups whipping cream
- 2½ cups dark chocolate, melted

CAKE
Using an electric mixer, cream the butter and sugar until pale and fluffy. Add the orange zest. While continuing to beat, add 5 of the eggs, one at a time.

Add half the ground hazelnuts and half the ground almonds. Add the remaining 4 eggs, one at a time. Mix in the remaining ground nuts. Fold in the melted chocolate until combined.

Divide the mixture between the prepared pans. Bake for 15 minutes, then reduce the oven temperature to 275°F and bake for a further 25–30 minutes, or until cooked when tested with a skewer. Allow the cakes to cool in the pans on a wire rack.

GANACHE FILLING AND FROSTING
Bring the cream just to a boil in a small saucepan. Remove from the heat and stir in the melted chocolate until smooth. Chill until the mixture is of a spreadable consistency.

To assemble, cover one cake with a thin layer of ganache, put the other cake on top, and use the rest of the ganache to glaze the side and top of the cake.

VARIATIONS
Use all almonds instead of a mixture of almonds and hazelnuts.

Omit the ganache, dust each cake with sifted confectioner's sugar and serve with whipped cream and seasonal berries.

Tip
- One cake can be frozen for future use.

SACHERTORTE

Coated with apricot jam and enrobed in chocolate ganache or glaze,
this famous cake was created in Vienna's Hotel Sacher in 1832.

SERVES 12–16

CAKE
7 oz unsalted butter, at room temperature ▪
7 oz superfine sugar ▪
8 large eggs, separated ▪
1¼ cups chopped dark chocolate, ▪
melted and cooled
1 teaspoon natural vanilla extract ▪
1⅔ cups self-rising flour ▪
2 tablespoons unsweetened cocoa powder, ▪
preferably Dutch style
⅓ cup apricot jam ▪

CHOCOLATE GLAZE
1 cup whipping cream ▪
1⅔ cups finely chopped dark chocolate ▪

Preheat the oven to 350°F. Butter a 10 inch round cake pan and line it with parchment paper.

CAKE
Using an electric mixer, cream the butter and two-thirds of the sugar until pale and fluffy. Beat in the egg yolks, one at a time. Stir in the chocolate and vanilla.

Using an electric mixer and clean, dry beaters, beat the egg whites until soft peaks form, then gradually add the remaining sugar and beat until stiff peaks form.

Sift the flour and cocoa together and fold into the chocolate mixture. Fold the meringue into the chocolate mixture in two additions. Pour into the prepared pan and bake for 40–50 minutes, or until cooked when tested with a skewer. Allow to cool in the pan on a wire rack for 10 minutes, then turn out onto the rack and allow to cool completely.

CHOCOLATE GLAZE
Bring the cream just to a boil, then pour it over the chopped chocolate. Allow to stand for 2–3 minutes, then stir gently until the chocolate has melted and the mixture is smooth. Allow to cool.

To assemble, carefully slice the cold cake in half horizontally.

Warm the apricot jam, then sieve it to remove any lumps. Brush half of the jam onto one cake layer. Place the other cake layer on top. Brush the top and side of the cake with the remaining jam. Pour the glaze over the cake and gently spread with a spatula.

If desired, spoon a little melted chocolate into a piping bag and use it to write 'Sacher' on top of the set glaze.

FLORENTINE CHEESECAKE

The ingredients characteristic of Florentine cookies—nuts, honey, and candied cherries—flavor the base of this unusual cheesecake.

SERVES 6

BASE
3 cups roughly crushed cornflakes ∎
¼ cup flaked almonds, toasted ∎
¼ cup flaked coconut, toasted ∎
1 tablespoon honey ∎
1 tablespoon chopped red candied cherries ∎
½ cup unsalted butter, melted ∎

FILLING
2 cups cream cheese, at room temperature ∎
½ cup superfine sugar ∎
1 cup whipping cream ∎
3 teaspoons powdered gelatin, dissolved in ∎
¼ cup boiling water
2 teaspoons grated orange zest ∎
¼ cup orange juice ∎
2 cups chopped white, milk or dark chocolate, melted ∎

Butter an 8 inch springform pan. Line the base and side with parchment paper.

BASE
Combine all the base ingredients in a bowl and mix well. Press the mixture evenly onto the base of the prepared pan. Chill for 10 minutes, or until firm.

FILLING
Using an electric mixer, beat the cream cheese and sugar until smooth. Add the cream and beat until thick and smooth. Fold in the gelatin mixture, orange zest, juice, and most of the melted chocolate, reserving some melted chocolate for decoration.

Pour the filling into the prepared base. Tap the pan on a work surface to even out the filling. Drizzle the cheesecake with the remaining melted chocolate. Chill for 2–3 hours, or until set.

WHITE CHOCOLATE MUD CAKE

This dense, moist cake is smothered in a delectable white chocolate ganache. It looks lovely decorated with candied orange peel; making your own candied peel is simple, and the result is far superior to the purchased variety.

SERVES 10–12

Preheat the oven to 325°F. Butter a 8 inch round cake pan and line it with parchment paper.

CAKE
1 cup unsalted butter ▪
9 oz superfine sugar ▪
½ cup lightly packed soft brown sugar ▪
¾ cup milk ▪
1½ cups chopped white chocolate ▪
2 cups all-purpose flour ▪
1 teaspoon baking powder ▪
2 large eggs, lightly beaten ▪
1 teaspoon natural vanilla extract ▪

WHITE CHOCOLATE GANACHE
½ cup whipping cream ▪
1 teaspoon light corn syrup ▪
2⅓ cups finely chopped white ▪
couverture chocolate

CANDIED ORANGE PEEL
Peel from 6–7 oranges (reserve the peel from oranges ▪
that have been squeezed for juice)
1¾ cups sugar ▪

CAKE
Place the butter, sugars, and milk in a saucepan over gentle heat and stir until the butter is melted. Place the chopped chocolate in a large mixing bowl. Pour the melted butter mixture over the chocolate, stir until smooth, then set aside to cool until tepid.

Sift the flour and baking powder together and stir into the cooled chocolate mixture. Whisk the eggs and vanilla and stir into the mixture. Pour into the prepared pan. Bake for 1–1¼ hours, or until cooked when tested with a skewer. If the cake begins to brown too much, cover it loosely with foil.

Allow the cake to cool in the pan on a wire rack before turning out.

WHITE CHOCOLATE GANACHE
In a small saucepan over medium heat, bring the cream and corn syrup just to boiling point. Put the chopped chocolate in a mixing bowl. Pour the hot cream over the chocolate (rather than adding the chocolate to the hot cream); this avoids 'splitting' the ganache.

Stir gently to combine, then refrigerate, stirring occasionally, until the mixture has thickened but is still of a flowing consistency; this will ensure a smooth covering. If the ganache becomes too cool, it can be swirled over the cake. Spread the cake with the ganache and decorate with candied orange peel if desired.

CANDIED ORANGE PEEL
Bring a saucepan of water to a boil. Add the orange peel, cover, and simmer for at least 1 hour. Drain and allow to cool. Using a spoon, scoop out the flesh and pith, leaving skin about ⅛ inch thick. Leave the skin as halves, or cut into strips, or dice depending on how you wish to use it.

Combine 2 cups water and the sugar in a saucepan and heat gently to dissolve the sugar. Boil for 1 minute. Add the peel to a boiling syrup and simmer for 20 minutes, or a little longer for larger pieces. The peel will become shiny and translucent. Remove from the heat and pack the orange peel into sterilized screw-top bottles. Pour the syrup over to cover and seal. Store in the refrigerator, or vacuum seal for a longer shelf life.

chapter nine

CHOCOLATE CELEBRATION

Life's special occasions, both large and small, deserve the accompaniment of celebratory dishes. This chapter presents a selection of festive chocolate cakes, from gorgeous wedding cakes to simpler cakes for family birthdays.

CHOCOLATE LOVERS' CELEBRATION CAKE

*A superb cake that can be simply dusted with sifted confectioner's sugar and served with whipped cream, or frosted as desired.
It can be baked in a heart-shaped pan, glazed with chocolate, and decorated with gold leaf and fresh red roses.*

SERVES 14

Soak the raisins in the whisky overnight.

2 cups raisins, chopped ■
½ cup Scotch whisky ■
2⅔ cups chopped dark chocolate ■
1 cup unsalted butter, chopped ■
6 large eggs, separated ■
1⅔ cups superfine sugar ■
2 cups self-rising flour ■
½ teaspoon ground nutmeg ■
1⅔ cups ground almonds, hazelnuts or pecans ■

Whipped cream or 1 quantity of Rich Chocolate Glaze ■
(page 226; optional), to serve

Preheat the oven to 325°F. Butter one 10 inch round, one 8½ inch square or two 8 inch round cake pan(s) and line them with parchment paper.

Melt the chocolate and butter in a heatproof bowl over hot water. Allow to cool.

Using an electric mixer, beat the egg yolks and sugar until pale and thick. Add the chocolate mixture and mix well. Transfer to a large mixing bowl. Fold in the sifted flour, nutmeg and ground nuts, then the whisky and raisin mixture.

Using clean, dry beaters, beat the egg whites until soft peaks form, then fold into the chocolate mixture in two batches. Mix well.

Pour the batter into the prepared pan(s). Bake for 1¼–1½ hours, or until cooked when tested with a skewer. Allow the cake(s) to cool in the pan(s) on a wire rack.

Serve with whipped cream or cover with Chocolate Glaze.

VARIATIONS
1 cup chopped pitted prunes (dried plums) can replace the raisins.

Brandy or dark rum may replace the whisky.

CHOCOLATE-ON-CHOCOLATE CAKE

This very moist cake has a delicate texture; it is best made two days before serving, to allow the flavors to mellow and the texture to mature.

SERVES 10

CAKE
1½ cups self-rising flour ▪
¼ cup unsweetened cocoa powder, ▪
preferably Dutch style
1 cup unsalted butter ▪
1 tablespoon instant coffee granules ▪
1 cup hot water ▪
1⅓ cups chopped dark chocolate ▪
2 cups superfine sugar ▪
2 large eggs, beaten ▪
1 teaspoon natural vanilla extract ▪

CHOCOLATE GLAZE
¾ cup chopped dark chocolate ▪
½ cup unsalted butter ▪

Preheat the oven to 315°F. Butter a 8 inch round cake pan and line it with parchment paper.

CAKE
Sift the flour and cocoa powder together.

Melt the butter in a large saucepan. Combine the instant coffee granules and hot water and add to the butter along with the chocolate and sugar. Stir until smooth. Remove from the heat and allow the mixture to cool.

Add the eggs and vanilla extract and beat well. Gently fold in the sifted dry ingredients, one-third at a time.

Pour the mixture into the prepared pan and bake for about 1½ hours, or until cooked when tested with a skewer. Allow to cool in the pan on a wire rack. When cold, remove from the pan and wrap well in foil until ready to serve.

CHOCOLATE GLAZE
Melt the chocolate and butter in a heatproof bowl over hot water. Allow to cool. Beat with a wooden spoon until thick and spreadable. Spread the glaze over the top and sides of the cake. Allow to set; this will take 1–2 hours depending on the weather. If in a hurry, place the glazed cake in the refrigerator for 10 minutes.

CHOCOLATE DOME

This striking cake can be made in stages for ease of preparation.
It looks particularly beautiful covered with fresh roses as a wedding cake.

SERVES 20

1 quantity Golden Sponge Cake or Chocolate Sponge Cake ■
(page 30), baked the day before in a jelly roll pan.
Slice the cold cake in half horizontally

SUGAR SYRUP
⅓ cup sugar ■
3 tablespoons liqueur or fruit juice ■

MOUSSE
2 cups chopped dark chocolate ■
3 large egg yolks ■
3¾ cups whipping cream ■
1 teaspoon natural vanilla extract ■
1 tablespoon powdered gelatin ■

GANACHE
1¼ cups whipping cream ■
2⅔ cups chopped dark chocolate, melted ■

Chocolate leaves (page 233), to decorate (optional) ■

Line a 12 cup bowl with foil or plastic wrap.

SUGAR SYRUP
Heat ⅔ cup water and the sugar in a small saucepan and bring to a boil, stirring constantly. Remove from the heat and stir in the liqueur or fruit juice. Allow to cool. Refrigerate in a sealed container until required.

MOUSSE
Put the chocolate in a heatproof bowl and melt it over a saucepan of hot water.

Whisk the egg yolks in a small heatproof bowl. Heat 1 cup of the cream in a small saucepan over low heat. Stir half the hot cream into the egg yolks. Return the mixture to the saucepan and stir with a wooden spoon over low heat until thickened. Strain into a clean bowl. Stir the melted chocolate into the hot custard. Add the vanilla and allow to cool until warm.

Dissolve the gelatin in ⅓ cup warm water and stir it into the warm chocolate custard. Whisk the remaining cream until soft peaks form. Fold into the chocolate mixture in two additions.

ASSEMBLY
First, cut a round from one half of the cake, using the upturned bowl as a mold. Set aside. Line the bowl with the rest of the sliced cake, trimming as necessary to fit the curve of the bowl, and sprinkle with half the sugar syrup. Pour the chocolate mousse mixture into the sponge-lined bowl. Refrigerate until set. Cover the surface with the reserved cake circle and sprinkle with more sugar syrup, reserving some syrup for frosting the cake. Cover and refrigerate overnight.

GANACHE
Bring the cream just to a boil in a small saucepan. Remove from the heat, add the melted chocolate and stir until smooth. Allow to cool until it is of a thick but still pourable consistency.

Unmold the cake onto a cake board, or onto a wire rack set over a baking sheet. Brush with the remaining syrup. Pour the ganache over the cake, spreading it with a spatula if necessary. Allow to set. Transfer to a serving plate and decorate with chocolate leaves.

FROSTED TIERED CHOCOLATE CAKE

*Although simple to make, this tiered cake is very impressive,
with a rich color due to the Dutch-style cocoa powder that it contains.*

SERVES 10–12

CAKE
1 cup unsweetened cocoa powder, ▪
preferably Dutch style
2 cups boiling water ▪
3 cups all-purpose flour ▪
2 teaspoons baking soda ▪
1/2 teaspoon baking powder ▪
1 cup unsalted butter, at room temperature ▪
21/4 cups superfine sugar ▪
4 large eggs ▪
11/2 teaspoons natural vanilla extract ▪

FROSTING
11/4 cups chopped dark chocolate ▪
1/2 cup whipping cream ▪
1 cup unsalted butter ▪
23/4 cups pure confectioner's sugar ▪

FILLING
11/4 cups whipping cream, chilled ▪
1/4 cup pure confectioner's sugar ▪
1 teaspoon natural vanilla extract ▪

Preheat the oven to 350°F. Butter three 8 inch round cake pans and line them with parchment paper.

CAKE
Blend the cocoa powder and boiling water in a small bowl until smooth. Allow to cool.

Sift the flour, baking soda, and baking powder together.

In the large bowl of an electric mixer, beat the butter, sugar, eggs, and vanilla extract on medium speed for about 5 minutes, or until pale and fluffy. With the mixer on low speed, add the flour mixture alternately with the cocoa mixture, ending with the flour mixture. Do not overbeat.

Divide the mixture evenly among the prepared pans and smooth the surface. Bake for 25–30 minutes, or until cooked when tested with a skewer. Allow to cool in the pans on wire racks for 10 minutes, then turn out onto the wire racks to cool completely.

FROSTING
Combine the chocolate, cream, and butter in a saucepan. Stir over medium heat until smooth. Remove from the heat. Whisk in the confectioner's sugar. Place the bowl over ice and beat the frosting with a wooden spoon until it is fluffy and holds its shape. Alternatively, allow the mixture to cool in the refrigerator, then beat with an electric mixer until fluffy.

FILLING
Beat the cream until stiff peaks form, then stir in the confectioner's sugar and vanilla extract. Refrigerate until needed.

ASSEMBLY AND DECORATION
Place one cake on a cake board and spread with half the cream filling. Position the second cake on top and spread with the remaining filling. Put the third cake in position. Using a spatula, first frost the sides of the cake with the frosting, then the top, swirling the frosting decoratively. Refrigerate for at least 1 hour before serving.

CHOCOLATE ALMOND CAKE

This cake can be served on its own, and also forms the foundation of Emma's Chocolate Almond Wedding Cake, opposite.

SERVES 8–10

2 cups chopped dark chocolate ■
7 oz unsalted butter, chopped ■
1 cup superfine sugar ■
6 large eggs, separated ■
⅔ cup all-purpose flour ■
1 teaspoon baking powder ■
¼ cup unsweetened cocoa powder, ■
preferably Dutch style
1¾ cups ground almonds ■

Preheat the oven to 325°F. Butter a deep 8 inch square cake pan, or a deep 9 inch round cake pan, and line it with parchment paper.

Melt the chocolate and butter in a large heatproof bowl set over a saucepan of hot water, stirring occasionally. Allow to cool.

Reserve one-third of the sugar. Add the remaining sugar to the egg yolks, beat with an electric mixer until pale, then add this to the chocolate mixture. Stir to combine.

Sift the flour, baking powder, cocoa powder, and ground almonds together. Using a rubber spatula, fold into the chocolate mixture.

Using clean beaters, beat the egg whites until soft peaks form, add the reserved sugar and beat until stiff and glossy but not dry. Using a rubber spatula, gently fold the egg whites into the chocolate mixture in two additions.

Pour the mixture into the prepared pan and bake for about 1 hour, or until cooked when tested with a skewer. Allow to cool in the pan for 10 minutes, then turn out onto a wire rack to cool completely.

VARIATION
This mixture can also be used to make 18 standard or 12 large cupcakes. Bake them for 30 minutes (for standard) or 35 minutes (for large) and decorate with the frosting of your choice.

EMMA'S CHOCOLATE ALMOND WEDDING CAKE

I developed this cake for Emma, my talented food stylist friend, who worked with me for many wonderful years.
Make the cakes 2-3 days in advance, wrap in plastic wrap, and store in an airtight container, not the refrigerator.

SERVES 32–40

4 quantities Chocolate Almond Cake (page 182), ■
baked in four 9 inch round cake pans
2 quantities Sugar Syrup (page 219) ■
2 quantities Chocolate Mousse Filling (page 223) ■
8 cups fresh raspberries ■
1 quantity White Chocolate Meringue Buttercream (page 221) ■

DECORATION (OPTIONAL)
Fresh unsprayed flowers ■
Chocolate roses and leaves made ■
from Dark Chocolate Plastic (page 235)

THE DAY BEFORE
Put each cake on a cake board and slice in half horizontally. Brush the cut side of each cake half with sugar syrup. Spread the bottom layer of each cake with a generous layer of chocolate mousse filling and sprinkle with fresh raspberries. Place the upper half of the cake on top. Refrigerate the four cakes separately until firm, about 1 hour.

To frost the cake, brush the top and sides of each cake with sugar syrup. Cover each cake with a thin layer of white chocolate meringue buttercream. This seals the cake, preventing crumbs, and gives the final frosting a 'clean' color. Refrigerate the cakes at this stage overnight.

ON THE DAY
It is advisable to assemble and decorate the cake stack at the wedding venue. To assemble, put the four cakes on top of one another. Cover the whole cake stack with white buttercream, using a plastic spatula. For a ribbon effect, use a flexible 11 inch wide metal spatula and make upward and downward strokes.

DECORATION
Roses and leaves may be molded by hand using Dark Chocolate Plastic. This can be done weeks in advance. Do not refrigerate.

If using fresh flowers (make sure they have not been sprayed), you will need a round of plastic, such as the upturned lid of a plastic takeaway container, and a piece of florists' foam (Oasis). Cut the foam to the shape of the plastic round. Secure the florists' foam to the plastic with double-sided tape. Moisten the foam with water. Secure the flowers in position, commencing from the outside in. Spray with water. Position on top of the cake.

VARIATION
Using White Chocolate Plastic (page 235), make thin ribbons about 1¼ inches wide through a hand-cranked pasta machine. Wrap the frosted cake with the ribbons.

ROASTED NUT CHOCOLATE PANFORTE

A speciality of Sienna, in Italy, panforte is a rich, spiced cake loaded with toasted nuts and dried fruit, which makes an excellent Christmas gift. It is best made at least two or three days before serving.

MAKES 2 CAKES; EACH CAKE SERVES 12

Edible rice paper sheets (see Tip) or parchment paper ■

1 cup hazelnuts ■
2 cups blanched almonds ■
2 cups unsalted macadamia nuts ■
3/4 cup unsalted raw pistachio nuts ■
1 cup candied or dried figs, thinly sliced ■
2 cups chopped dark chocolate ■
1 3/4 cups honey ■
1/2 cup superfine sugar ■
1 1/2 cups all-purpose flour ■
2 tablespoons unsweetened cocoa powder, ■
preferably Dutch style
2 teaspoons ground cinnamon ■
1/2 teaspoon grated nutmeg ■

Sifted pure confectioner's sugar ■
or cocoa powder, for decoration

Preheat the oven to 315°F. Butter two 8 inch round cake pans and line them with rice paper or parchment paper (if using rice paper, you may need to overlap the sheets depending on their size).

Put the hazelnuts, almonds, macadamias, and pistachios on baking sheets, keeping each type of nut separate, and toast in the oven for about 7 minutes, or until pale golden. Rub the hot hazelnuts in a clean cloth to remove the skins (not all of the skins will come off; don't worry about those that remain).

Combine the hot nuts and sliced figs.

Melt the chocolate in a heatproof bowl over hot water.

In a heavy-based saucepan, gently heat the honey and sugar until the sugar dissolves. Bring to a boil and remove from the heat. Add the melted chocolate and beat well using a wooden spoon.

Stir the flour, cocoa, and spices into the nut and flour mixture, stir to mix, then add the chocolate and honey syrup. Working quickly, mix well; the mixture will be very stiff. Press into the prepared pans, using a wet hand if necessary to smooth out the surface.

Bake for 45–50 minutes, or until the cake is firm-looking and coming away from the sides of the pans. It will also give off a strong honey aroma when cooked. Cool in the pans on a wire rack.

Store in an airtight container. To serve, dust with sifted confectioner's sugar or cocoa powder.

VARIATIONS
Replace the figs with 1 cup finely chopped candied apricots, or 1 cup finely chopped pitted prunes (dried plums).

A WHITE CHOCOLATE VERSION
Replace the dark chocolate with white chocolate, and add 1 tablespoon candied ginger, chopped dried cherries, and 5 3/4 cups of combined nuts of your choice.

Tip
■ Rice paper is an edible, flavorless, translucent paper available from cake decorating stores, Asian markets, or health food stores.

CHRISTMAS ICE-CREAM BOMBE

This frozen pudding is an ideal hot-climate replacement for the traditional steamed pudding. It can be made a week ahead and kept frozen. Although a dome shape is traditional for a bombe, an alternative is to freeze the mixture in a log pan.

SERVES 10–15

1 quantity Classic Chocolate Ice Cream (page 118), ■
churned until thickened but not frozen

FRUITED ICE CREAM
1/3 cup red and green candied cherries, ■
or sweetened dried cranberries (craisins)
1/3 cup chopped mixed peel or ■
Candied Orange Peel (page 172)
1/3 cup raisins, chopped ■
1/3 cup golden raisins ■
1/3 cup currants ■
1 teaspoon ground cinnamon ■
1 teaspoon ground nutmeg ■
1 tablespoon brandy, rum or sherry ■
1 tablespoon hot water ■
21 fl oz whipping cream ■
3/4 cup pure confectioner's sugar, sifted ■
1 tablespoon unsweetened cocoa powder, ■
preferably Dutch style
5 large egg whites ■
1/4 teaspoon cream of tartar ■

TOPPING (OPTIONAL)
3/4 cup chopped dark chocolate ■
1/4 cup whipping cream ■
Holly sprigs and 1 candied cherry, to decorate ■

Line the inside of a 12 cup bowl with plastic wrap and chill. Gently spoon the thickened ice cream over the inside of the lined bowl to form a shell.

Cover the outside of a slightly smaller bowl with plastic wrap. Place this bowl inside the other to help the ice cream mold to the right shape. Freeze until set, or overnight.

FRUITED ICE CREAM
Combine the fruits, spices, alcohol, and water and allow the fruit to soak for 3 hours, or overnight.

Beat the cream until thick, then add half the confectioner's sugar and the cocoa. Stir the fruit and its soaking liquid into the cream mixture.

Using clean beaters, whisk the egg whites and cream of tartar until stiff peaks form. Beat in the remaining confectioner's sugar. Gently fold the egg whites into the fruit mixture until combined.

Remove the plastic-wrapped inner bowl and pour the fruited ice-cream mixture into the frozen ice-cream shell. Freeze overnight.

To serve, turn out onto a serving plate and carefully peel away the plastic wrap, then cut into slices or wedges.

TOPPING
If making the topping, melt the chocolate with the cream over low heat. Remove from the heat and allow to cool, then pour over the top of the unmolded bombe. Decorate with a candied cherry and holly sprigs, if desired.

DARK CHOCOLATE FUDGE CAKE

This basic cake makes one cake layer; make multiple layers for a tiered wedding or birthday cake.
Bake the cake two days in advance.

SERVES 10

- 1 cup unsalted butter, chopped ∎
- 1⅔ cups chopped dark chocolate ∎
- 1⅓ cups superfine sugar ∎
- 6 large eggs, separated ∎
- ¾ cup all-purpose flour ∎
- ¾ cup self-rising flour ∎
- ¼ cup unsweetened cocoa powder, preferably Dutch style ∎
- 1 teaspoon natural vanilla extract ∎

Preheat the oven to 350°F. Butter a 9–10 inch round cake pan and line with parchment paper.

Melt the butter and the chocolate in a saucepan over low heat. Remove from the heat and stir until smooth.

Reserve 2 tablespoons of the sugar. Add the remaining sugar to the chocolate mixture and mix well. Add the egg yolks, one by one, and mix well.

Sift the flours and cocoa powder together and gently fold the dry ingredients into the chocolate mixture.

Using an electric mixer, beat the egg whites until soft peaks form. Add the reserved sugar and beat for 2–3 minutes, or until the mixture is thick and the sugar has dissolved. Fold into the chocolate mixture in two additions. Fold in the vanilla extract.

Pour the mixture into the prepared pan. Bake for 40–45 minutes, or until cooked when tested with a skewer.

Allow to cool in the pan for 10 minutes, then remove carefully and transfer to a wire rack to cool completely.

Tips

- If the surface has cracked during baking, use your fingers to push down the cake surface as it cools. Any imperfections can be concealed with frosting or glaze.
- Store the cake in a cool place, but do not refrigerate.
- The cake can be split, brushed with liqueur-flavored sugar syrup, then filled with mousse, ganache, or sour cherry conserve.

RICH CHOCOLATE FRUIT CAKE

This cake is suitable as a Christmas or wedding cake, and will keep beautifully for several months, during which time its flavors will mellow and improve. While still hot, the cooked cake can be generously brushed with extra brandy.

SERVES 24

1²/₃ cups raisins, chopped ▪
2 cups golden raisins ▪
²/₃ cup currants ▪
½ cup chopped candied cherries ▪
4½ oz Candied Orange Peel (page 172), chopped ▪
½ cup chopped candied figs ▪
2 tablespoons chopped candied ginger ▪
½ cup chopped pitted dates ▪
½ cup brandy, plus extra for brushing (optional) ▪
1 cup unsalted butter, at room temperature ▪
1⅓ cups lightly packed soft brown sugar ▪
5 large eggs ▪
1 tablespoon light corn syrup or honey ▪
1 tablespoon marmalade or apricot jam ▪
2 cups all-purpose flour ▪
½ cup self-rising flour ▪
½ teaspoon ground cinnamon ▪
¼ teaspoon ground nutmeg ▪
2 tablespoons unsweetened cocoa powder, preferably Dutch style, sifted ▪
½ cup ground almonds ▪
1 cup chopped dark chocolate ▪

Mix all the fruits together in a large bowl, add the brandy, cover and allow to macerate for 1–2 days, stirring occasionally.

Preheat the oven to 310°F. Butter a deep 8 inch square or 9 inch round cake pan, line it with a double thickness of brown paper, then butter the paper.

Using an electric mixer, cream the butter and sugar until pale and fluffy. Add the eggs, one at a time, beating well after each addition. Beat in the light corn syrup or honey and marmalade or jam.

Sift the flours, spices, cocoa, and ground almonds together. Using a wooden spoon, stir half the flour into the creamed mixture. Add the remaining flour and mix well.

Lastly, stir in the fruit mixture and the chopped chocolate. Spoon the mixture into the prepared pan and smooth the surface. Bake for 1 hour, then reduce the oven temperature to 275°F and bake for a further 2½ hours, or until cooked when tested with a skewer. Cover loosely with foil during the last stages of baking to prevent any excess browning.

While the cake is still hot, brush with extra brandy if desired. Allow to cool completely in the pan. Turn out and wrap in foil to store.

Tip
▪ Instead of the variety of fruits specified above, use up to 2 lb 4 oz of whatever dried fruits you wish.

MIETTA'S CHOCOLATE WEDDING CAKE

Mietta O'Donnell was a renowned Australian restaurateur. This celebration chocolate cake has been a favorite of her family for decades, and I have included it here in her memory.

SERVES 10 AS A DESSERT, 20 WITH COFFEE

CAKE
6 large eggs, lightly beaten ▪
3/4 cup superfine sugar ▪
1½ cups all-purpose flour ▪
¼ cup unsweetened cocoa powder, ▪
preferably Dutch style

COATING
2 cups whipping cream ▪
5 cups finely chopped dark chocolate ▪

RUM SYRUP
⅓ cup water ▪
⅓ cup sugar ▪
⅓ cup dark rum ▪

DECORATION
Chocolate curls or rolls (page 233), made from 5½ oz ▪
dark or white chocolate

Make the cake the day before you want to decorate it. Preheat the oven to 400°F. Butter a deep 10 inch round cake pan and line it with parchment paper.

CAKE
Put the eggs and sugar in a heatproof bowl over a saucepan of simmering water and stir until warm. Remove from the heat and beat with an electric mixer on high speed for 8–10 minutes, or until pale, thick, and tripled in volume.

Sift the flour and cocoa powder together. Add to the egg mixture and fold through using a rubber spatula. Pour into the prepared pan and bake for 20–25 minutes. Allow to cool completely in the pan, then turn out gently onto a wire rack.

COATING
Put the cream in a heavy-based saucepan and bring quickly to a boil, boil for 1 minute, then remove from the heat. Add the chopped chocolate, allow to stand for 1 minute, then stir until smooth. Allow to stand, stirring occasionally, until of a spreadable consistency.

RUM SYRUP
Bring the water and sugar to a boil in a small, heavy-based saucepan. Boil gently for 2–3 minutes, until the sugar is dissolved. Allow to cool, then add the rum. Refrigerate until required.

ASSEMBLY
Cut the chocolate cake horizontally into three layers. Brush one layer generously with a third of the rum syrup, then gently spread on a 1/16 inch thick layer of the chocolate coating. Repeat with the other rounds of cake, stacking them, then cover the entire cake with the rest of the chocolate coating. Refrigerate for 1 hour before serving.

Tip
▪ The quantity can be increased and the recipe adapted for a wedding cake; for variation, try covering the cake with White Chocolate Ganache (page 172) and decorating it with chocolate curls or rolls (page 233).

APRICOT AND PECAN WHITE CHRISTMAS CAKE

Inspiration for this delicious cake came from a recipe given to me by Beverley Sutherland Smith.

SERVES 24

- 2 cups candied apricots, finely chopped
- 1 cup golden raisins
- 2½ cups pecans, roughly chopped
- 2 cups all-purpose flour
- 1 cup unsalted butter, at room temperature
- 1⅓ cups superfine sugar
- Grated zest of 2 oranges
- Grated zest of 1 lemon
- 5 large eggs
- ½ teaspoon baking powder
- 1⅓ cups chopped white chocolate, melted
- 2 tablespoons orange liqueur or brandy, plus a little extra for brushing (optional)

Preheat the oven to 325°F. Butter a deep 9 inch round or 8 inch square cake pan and line it with parchment paper. Wrap the pan in foil to prevent the outside of the cake from browning too much.

Mix the apricots, sultanas, and pecans in a bowl. Add ¼ cup of the flour to the fruit and mix so that it is coated.

Using an electric mixer, cream the butter and sugar together until pale and fluffy. Add the orange and lemon zests, then beat in the eggs one at a time.

Sift the remaining flour with the baking powder and mix into the creamed mixture. Fold in the cooled melted chocolate and liqueur or brandy.

Stir in the fruits and mix well. Spoon the mixture into the prepared pan. Bake for about 1½ hours, or until cooked when tested with a skewer. Cover the cake loosely with a piece of foil during the last stages of baking if the surface is browning too much.

Brush the hot cake with extra liqueur or brandy, if desired. Allow to cool completely in the pan before turning out. Wrap the cake in foil before storing.

chapter ten

CHOCOLATE IN MINIATURE

The aesthetic appeal of bite-sized morsels is undeniable. Fudge, meringues,
macaroons, truffles, and rum balls — such tiny treats are ideal for afternoon tea;
or, for a different style of dessert, serve a selection of them as a tasting platter.
As a bonus, these little delicacies present beautifully, making them ideal as edible gifts.

NUT AND CHOCOLATE NOUGAT

This honey-flavored French candy is dense with almonds, pistachios, and hazelnuts. The nuts may be chopped or left whole. You will need a strong electric mixer for this recipe; a hand mixer may not be robust enough.

MAKES 48 MEDIUM OR 60 SMALL PIECES

4 sheets edible rice paper (see Tip) ■
3¼ cups almonds ■
⅔ cup hazelnuts ■
¾ cup pistachio nuts ■
7 fl oz corn syrup ■
1¾ cups white sugar ■
1 lb 2 oz honey ■
2½ large egg whites ■
2 tablespoons superfine sugar ■
1 cup chopped dark chocolate, melted ■

Preheat the oven to 300°F. Line a 9 x 13 inch x 2 inch deep cake pan with parchment paper. Put two sheets of rice paper, rough side up, in the pan.

Put the nuts on parchment paper on a baking sheet and toast in the oven for 10 minutes, stirring occasionally. Reduce the oven temperature to 200°F and keep the nuts warm.

Meanwhile, put ½ cup water, the corn syrup, and granulated sugar in a saucepan over low heat. Stir to dissolve the sugar, brushing down the side of the pan with a pastry brush dipped in water. Once the sugar is dissolved, bring the mixture to a boil. Once boiling, do not stir, as this may crystallize the syrup. Heat to 285°F (soft-crack stage) on a sugar thermometer.

Meanwhile, heat the honey to 275–285°F (soft-crack stage). At the same time, beat the egg whites to firm peaks in the large bowl of an electric mixer. Beating on low speed, gradually add the superfine sugar.

Pour the hot honey and then the sugar syrup onto the egg whites in a steady stream, while beating on low speed. (To prevent spatters, avoid pouring the hot mixture onto the beaters.) Increase the speed to medium–high and beat for 5 minutes, then beat on low speed for 5 minutes more. Gradually the mixture will become pale and very thick, forming thick ribbons when the beaters are lifted.

Using a strong wooden spoon, fold in the hot nuts and cooled melted chocolate. You will need to work quickly, as the mixture will harden rapidly at this stage; if possible, get a strong friend to help you mix it. Spoon the nougat into the prepared pan. Cover with the remaining sheets of rice paper, rough side down. Smooth it flat with your hands, or roll with a small rolling pin if you have one.

Allow the nougat to cool completely (do not refrigerate). Loosen the sides of the nougat, prising them away from the pan, then turn out onto a chopping board. Slice with a large serrated knife.

Tip
■ Rice paper is an edible, flavorless, translucent paper available from cake decorating stores, Asian markets or health food stores.

CHOCOLATE HAZELNUT CRESCENTS

These delicate horseshoe-shaped Italian cookies are ideal to serve with coffee.
The recipe was developed by my good friend Von Canty.

MAKES 24

2½ cups all-purpose flour, sifted ■
½ cup superfine sugar ■
1 cup unsalted butter, chilled and chopped ■
¼ cup hazelnuts, toasted, skinned (see opposite), ■
cooled and ground; or use ready-ground hazelnuts
½ cup finely chopped dark chocolate ■
1 large egg yolk ■
Pure confectioner's sugar or cocoa powder, for dusting ■

Preheat the oven to 325°F. Lightly butter two baking sheets.

Sift the flour and sugar into a bowl. Rub the butter into the flour mixture (or process in a food processor) until it resembles breadcrumbs, then add the ground nuts, chocolate, and egg yolk. Mix or process until combined. Turn out onto a lightly floured surface and knead lightly until the dough comes together into a ball.

Roll the dough into a log shape and divide into 24 portions. Roll each portion into a fat sausage about 3¼ inches long, then bend to form a crescent. Place on the prepared sheet and bake for 15 minutes, or until lightly browned.

Cool on the sheet for about 5 minutes, toss in sifted confectioner's sugar while still hot, then transfer to a wire rack to cool completely.

HAZELNUT COOKIES

For variation, almonds can replace the hazelnuts.

MAKES 50

1⅓ cups hazelnuts, toasted (see Note) ▪
2½ cups all-purpose flour ▪
1 teaspoon baking powder ▪
⅓ cup unsweetened cocoa powder, ▪
preferably Dutch style
1 cup unsalted butter, at room temperature ▪
1¼ cups pure confectioner's sugar, sifted ▪
2 large eggs, lightly beaten ▪
⅔ cup grated dark chocolate ▪
Superfine sugar, for rolling ▪

Preheat the oven to 350°F. Lightly butter baking sheets.

Chop the hazelnuts coarsely.

Sift together the flour, baking powder, and cocoa powder.

Using an electric mixer, cream the butter and confectioner's sugar until pale and fluffy. Add the eggs, beat well, then fold in the sifted dry ingredients. Fold in the grated chocolate and chopped hazelnuts.

Divide the mixture into three equal portions. Roll each portion to form a log with a 1 inch diameter, then roll in superfine sugar. Wrap in plastic wrap and freeze for 2 hours, or until firm.

Remove the cookie dough from the freezer and cut into ½ inch slices. Put onto the prepared sheets, allowing room for spreading. Bake for 12–15 minutes, or until cooked. Allow to cool on the sheets for a few minutes, then transfer to a wire rack. The cookies will become crisp as they cool.

Store in an airtight container.

NOTE To toast hazelnuts, place them on parchment paper on a baking sheet and toast in the oven for 6–8 minutes, shaking the sheet from time to time. Remove, place in a clean dish towel, gather up the corners to form a parcel, and rub vigorously to remove the skins (not all of the skins will come off; don't worry about those that remain).

Tip
▪ After each slice, give the roll a slight turn; this prevents it from being flattened by always being cut from the same side.

CARAMEL BAR COOKIE

Caramel and chocolate are a truly luscious combination. This versatile bar cookie may be served in tiny squares to enjoy as petits fours with after-dinner coffee, or cut into larger pieces for afternoon tea.

MAKES 96 PETITS FOURS (1 INCH SQUARE) OR 24 LARGER PIECES (2 INCHES SQUARE)

BASE
½ cup unsalted butter
1 cup firmly packed soft brown sugar
1 cup grated dried coconut
1 cup self-rising flour

CARAMEL FILLING
1¼ cups sweetened condensed milk
2 tablespoons golden syrup, or 1 tablespoon corn syrup
1 oz unsalted butter

TOPPING
1⅓ cups chopped dark chocolate

Preheat the oven to 350°F. Butter a 9 x 13 inch cake pan and line it with parchment paper, extending the paper over two sides of the pan for easy removal later.

BASE
Melt the butter in a saucepan. Mix in the brown sugar, coconut, and sifted flour and press into the prepared pan. Bake for 10–15 minutes, or until cooked and slightly browned. Allow to cool.

CARAMEL FILLING
Combine the condensed milk, golden syrup or corn syrup, and butter in a saucepan. Stir constantly and gently over low–medium heat, to prevent the mixture from catching on the bottom of the pan, for about 5 minutes, or until thickened.

Spread evenly over the cooled, cooked base. Bake in the oven for 10 minutes, or until small bubbles appear. Allow to cool completely in the pan.

TOPPING
Once the bar cookie is thoroughly cooled, melt the chocolate and spread over the caramel mix. Allow to set.

Remove from the pan and cut into four pieces, cleaning the knife after each cut. Trim the edges. Cut each quarter into about 24 tiny portions if making petits fours, or six larger pieces if serving for afternoon tea.

VARIATION
For a thicker caramel layer, double the quantity of condensed milk, golden syrup, and butter.

Tips
- Clean the knife before each cut by dipping in hot water, then wiping it dry.
- The base mixture and the caramel filling can be baked the day before the bar cookie is to be frosted.

CHOCOLATE AND GINGER MERINGUES

The hot piquancy of ginger teams well with the richness of chocolate in these tiny morsels.

MAKES 40 MERINGUE SANDWICHES

MERINGUES
4 large egg whites ■
9 oz superfine sugar ■
2/3 cup unsweetened cocoa powder, ■
preferably Dutch style
1/4 cup candied ginger in syrup, ■
drained and finely chopped

CHOCOLATE GANACHE
3½ fl oz whipping cream ■
1 cup chopped dark or milk chocolate, melted ■
2 tablespoons unsalted butter, at room temperature ■

Preheat the oven to 225°F. Line two baking sheets with parchment paper.

MERINGUES
Using an electric mixer, beat the egg whites until stiff peaks form. Gradually add half the sugar, beating continuously on high speed for 2–3 minutes, or until very stiff and glossy.

Using a rubber spatula, fold in the remaining sugar mixed with the sifted cocoa powder until combined. Lastly, fold in the ginger.

Place the meringue into a large piping bag fitted with a plain ½ inch nozzle. Twist the bag to seal. Pipe small mounds onto the prepared baking sheets, allowing room for spreading. Alternatively, place teaspoons of meringue on the sheets.

Bake for 1 hour. Turn off the heat and leave in the oven until cool.

CHOCOLATE GANACHE
Bring the cream to a boil in a small saucepan. Remove from the heat, add the melted chocolate and stir thoroughly. Cool to tepid and gently stir in the butter. Chill the mixture until firm.

ASSEMBLY
Pair the meringues according to size. Sandwich each pair with the chocolate ganache and place into small paper liners. Chill until ready to serve.

RICH CHOCOLATE FUDGE

Although quite delectable just as it is, this fudge can, if you wish, be topped with a ganache or frosting and sprinkled with chopped nuts before it is cut into pieces.

MAKES ABOUT 74 SMALL PIECES

1⅓ cups sugar ▪
1 cup corn syrup ▪
1 cup whipping cream ▪
1¾ oz unsalted butter ▪
1⅔ cups chopped dark chocolate ▪

Line a shallow 8 inch square cake pan with parchment paper.

Combine the sugar, corn syrup, and cream in a heavy-based saucepan and stir over low heat until the sugar dissolves. Bring to a boil, then increase the heat to medium and cook, stirring, until the mixture reaches 239°F (soft-ball stage) on a sugar thermometer.

Remove from the heat and cool to 212°F. Add the butter and chocolate and stir until smooth. Pour into the prepared pan and allow to set at room temperature for 24 hours. Do not refrigerate.

When the fudge is firm, cut with a sharp knife into pieces about 1¼ inches square.

NOTE If you do not have a sugar thermometer, the temperature of a boiled sugar syrup can be gauged by dropping a small amount of the mixture (about ⅓ teaspoon) into a glass of cold water and seeing how the mixture reacts.

If the mixture forms a ball that flattens of its own accord, it has reached soft-ball stage. A ball that holds its shape indicates firm-ball stage, and a ball that is hard and firm indicates hard-ball stage.

If the mixture forms hard, pliable threads, soft-crack stage has been reached; hard, brittle threads indicate hard-crack stage.

VARIATIONS

WHITE CHOCOLATE
Replace the dark chocolate with 1¾ cups finely chopped or grated white chocolate.

MILK CHOCOLATE
Replace the dark chocolate with 1⅔ cups finely chopped or grated milk chocolate.

OTHER VARIATIONS
Chopped nuts or dried fruits may be added after the grated chocolate has been added.

CARAMEL CHOCOLATE ALMONDS

These crunchy delicacies are best eaten on the day they are made.

MAKES 18–20

1⅓ cups blanched almonds ▪
1⅓ cups superfine sugar ▪
1 cup roughly chopped dark chocolate ▪

Lightly butter a baking sheet.

Put the almonds and sugar in a saucepan over medium heat and stir with a wooden spoon until the sugar caramelizes and the almonds are golden.

Working quickly, spoon the mixture, using two dessertspoons, onto the baking sheet in flat clusters. Set aside to cool.

Melt the chocolate gently in a heatproof bowl over hot water. Remove from the heat and allow to cool slightly.

Stir until smooth, then dip half of each almond cluster into the melted chocolate. Allow the excess to drip back into the bowl, then put the cluster on a piece of parchment paper and allow to set.

RUM BALLS

Intensely chocolatey and heady with rum, these tiny confections are always popular.

MAKES ABOUT 40

2 cups chopped dark chocolate ▪
2 cups pure confectioner's sugar, sifted, ▪
plus extra for dusting
2 teaspoons instant coffee granules ▪
1⅔ cups ground almonds ▪
2 tablespoons whipping cream ▪
2 tablespoons dark rum ▪
½ cup unsweetened cocoa powder and ▪
⅓ cup pure confectioner's sugar,
sifted together, for coating

1⅔ cups chopped dark chocolate, tempered,▪
for dipping (optional)

Melt the chocolate in a heatproof bowl over a saucepan of hot water. Add the confectioner's sugar, coffee granules, ground almonds, cream, and rum and mix well.

Cover the mixture and refrigerate until firm.

Roll the mixture into small balls and toss in the combined sifted cocoa and confectioner's sugar. Alternatively, dip in the melted chocolate.

CHOCOLATE MACAROONS

Macaroons are delicate little nut-based meringue cookies. Here, they are sandwiched together with rich ganache.

MAKES 35–40
SANDWICHED MACAROONS

MACAROONS
1½ cups ground almonds ▪
2½ cups pure confectioner's sugar ▪
1¾ oz unsweetened cocoa powder, ▪
preferably Dutch style
4 large egg whites ▪
3 tablespoons superfine sugar ▪

CHOCOLATE GANACHE FILLING
7 fl oz whipping cream ▪
1⅔ cups finely chopped dark chocolate ▪
¼ cup unsalted butter, chopped, at room temperature ▪

Preheat the oven to 350°F. Line baking sheets with parchment paper.

MACAROONS
Sift the ground almonds, confectioner's sugar, and cocoa powder into the large bowl of an electric mixer. Using the whisk attachment, whisk on low speed, scraping down the sides of the bowl, until the ingredients are thoroughly combined. Pass the mixture through a sieve onto parchment paper.

Using clean, dry beaters, whisk the egg whites until soft peaks form, then gradually add the sugar, whisking for 1 minute, or until the mixture is glossy and firm peaks form.

Using a rubber spatula, very gently fold the almond mixture into the whipped egg whites, one-third at a time. The mixture will lose volume at this stage. Transfer the mixture to a piping bag fitted with a plain nozzle slightly larger than ½ inch in diameter. Set aside for 5 minutes; this allows the mixture to 'relax' and soften, making piping easier.

Pipe the macaroon paste in small mounds onto the prepared sheets, allowing room for spreading. Bake until puffed and crusted a little, 10–12 minutes. Allow to cool on the sheets for a few minutes, then transfer to a wire rack to cool completely.

CHOCOLATE GANACHE FILLING
Bring the cream to a boil, remove from the heat, and add the chocolate. Allow to stand, to soften the chocolate, then stir in the butter until the mixture is smooth. Chill for about 30 minutes, or until the filling is firm but still spreadable.

When the macaroons are cool, sandwich them together with the chocolate ganache filling.

Tip
▪ Any leftover ganache can be formed into walnut-sized balls, tossed in sifted confectioner's sugar and cocoa powder and served as truffles.

ORANGE CHOCOLATE DELIGHTS

*Although by no means difficult to make, these delicate confections are very impressive looking,
and are ideal to serve with coffee as an after-dinner treat.*

MAKES 40

MINI CHOCOLATE CUPS
Vegetable oil spray ▪
2²/₃ cups chopped dark chocolate, melted ▪

ORANGE CREAM FILLING
1 teaspoon powdered gelatin ▪
1 cup cream cheese, at room temperature ▪
½ cup mascarpone cheese ▪
Grated zest of 1 orange ▪
2 teaspoons pure confectioner's sugar, sifted ▪
2 tablespoons orange liqueur or brandy ▪

Grated dark chocolate, to decorate ▪

MINI CHOCOLATE CUPS
You will need 40 tiny paper liners for this recipe. Lightly spray the paper liners with vegetable oil. Using the melted chocolate, line each case with 1½ teaspoons of chocolate, running the back of the spoon twice around the side of each case to strengthen it.

Put the cups in the refrigerator for 5 minutes to set.

ORANGE CREAM FILLING
In a small bowl, soften the gelatin in 1 tablespoon cold water, then place over a bowl of hot water and stir gently until the gelatin is dissolved.

Put the cream cheese, mascarpone cheese, dissolved gelatin, orange zest, confectioner's sugar, and liqueur or brandy in a bowl and beat until combined.

Put the mixture into a pastry bag fitted with a star nozzle and pipe it into the chocolate cups. Decorate with grated chocolate and refrigerate until ready to serve.

Tips
- ▪ Do not store the confections for a long time in the refrigerator, or moisture will form on them. As the filling is perishable, the filled cups should be eaten within a day. Unfilled cups will last up to a month in an airtight container at room temperature.
- ▪ Using tempered chocolate (see page 14) will give a mirror sheen to the chocolate cups, and avoids the possibility of 'bloom' developing.

CLASSIC CHOCOLATE TRUFFLES

To the chocolate lover, truffles are the ultimate indulgence. They look very enticing tossed in cocoa powder or dipped in melted couverture chocolate, then served in pretty, tiny paper liners.

MAKES 60

1½ cups unsweetened cocoa powder, preferably Dutch style
3⅓ cups chopped dark chocolate
1 cup whipping cream
¼ cup orange or raspberry liqueur, or brandy

2⅔ cups chopped dark chocolate, melted, for dipping (optional)

Line a baking sheet with parchment paper and dust it with some of the sifted cocoa powder.

Put the chocolate in a large heatproof bowl and stand it over a saucepan of hot water, stirring occasionally as it melts.

Put the cream in a saucepan and bring gently to a boil. Allow to cool, then pour the cream through a fine sieve onto the melted chocolate and stir until blended. Add the liqueur and stir through. Chill the mixture in a bowl over iced water until it has thickened, 30–60 minutes. Alternatively, chill it in the refrigerator, stirring from time to time.

Beat the mixture with an electric mixer (if using a stand mixer, use the paddle attachment) until it lightens in color and thickens, about 30 seconds. Do not over-beat, or the mixture will harden.

Fit a pastry bag with a ½ inch round piping tip. Fill the bag with the truffle mixture. Pipe onto the prepared baking sheet, forming small balls about 1 inch wide, and then sprinkle with sifted cocoa powder. Alternatively, form them into rough balls using two teaspoons for a 'rustic' effect. (You may not need all of the cocoa powder, depending on how thickly you coat the truffles.)

Allow to set in a cool place until firm. Do not refrigerate.

If desired, dip the formed truffles, one at a time, into the tepid melted chocolate. Re-dip each truffle, then toss in more sifted cocoa powder, if desired. Allow to set on clean parchment paper.

CHOCOLATE CUPCAKES

Remember those old-fashioned cupcakes Grandma made? Whether frosted and decorated with sprinkles, or with their tops cut into wings to make fairy cakes, these are always a hit at children's parties.

MAKES 12–14

¾ cup unsalted butter, at room temperature ▪
1 cup superfine sugar ▪
⅔ cup chopped dark chocolate, melted ▪
and cooled to tepid
2 large eggs, beaten ▪
1½ cups all-purpose flour ▪
2 teaspoons baking powder ▪
1 tablespoon unsweetened cocoa powder, ▪
preferably Dutch style
½–¾ cup milk ▪

Preheat the oven to 350°F. Line a standard muffin pan with paper liners.

Cream the butter and sugar until pale and fluffy. Beat in the cooled melted chocolate. Add the beaten egg and beat until smooth.

Sift the flour, baking powder, and cocoa together. Fold the dry ingredients into the chocolate mixture in two additions, alternating with the milk. Use ½ cup of the milk to start with, adding more if necessary to give a light mixture.

Divide the mixture among the paper liners, filling each about three-quarters full. Bake for 18–20 minutes, or until well risen and cooked.

Cool for 10 minutes in the pan, then remove and transfer to a wire rack. Frost or decorate when cold.

VARIATIONS
FAIRY CAKES OR BUTTERFLIES
When the cakes are cold, use a small knife to cut a 'cap' from the top of each cupcake. Slice each cap in half to form the wings. Fill the center of the cake with whipped cream, then place the wings on top at an angle. Dust with sifted confectioner's sugar before serving.

CHOCOLATE CHERRY CUPCAKES
Fold in ½ cup pitted, chopped cherries into the base mixture. Frost with chocolate frosting and decorate with a fresh or candied cherry.

PRUNE AND HAZELNUT SQUARES

Prunes go particularly well with port or brandy. Here, the combination features in an indulgent chocolate delicacy that's ideal to serve with after-dinner coffee.

MAKES ABOUT 20

½ cup pitted prunes (dried plums), chopped ▪
¼ cup good-quality port or brandy ▪
⅔ cup toasted hazelnuts,
skins removed, chopped ▪
¼ cup whipping cream ▪
2 cups chopped dark chocolate, melted ▪

Line a 7 inch square cake pan with parchment paper, extending the paper over two sides of the pan to allow for easy removal later.

Combine the prunes and port or brandy, and allow to soak overnight, then add the toasted hazelnuts to the prune mixture.

Heat the cream in a small, heavy-based saucepan until boiling. Remove from the heat and stir in the melted chocolate and the prune and nut mixture.

Pour into the prepared pan, refrigerate for 10 minutes, then allow to set at room temperature, preferably overnight.

Slice into tiny squares and serve with coffee.

VARIATION
Toasted almonds or walnuts may be substituted for hazelnuts.

TINY MERINGUES WITH ALMONDS
AND CHOCOLATE CREAM

MAKES 30 SANDWICHED MERINGUES

MERINGUE
2 large egg whites ∎
4½ oz superfine sugar ∎
½ cup flaked almonds ∎

CHOCOLATE CREAM
½ cup whipping cream ∎
⅔ cup chopped dark or milk chocolate, ∎
melted and cooled to tepid
1½ teaspoons pure confectioner's sugar, sifted ∎
1½ teaspoons brandy or 1 teaspoon natural vanilla extract ∎

Preheat the oven to 225°F. Line two baking sheets with parchment paper.

MERINGUE
Beat the egg whites until stiff peaks form. Gradually add half the sugar, beating continuously, until the mixture is very stiff and glossy. Using a rubber spatula, fold in the remaining sugar.

Place the meringue mixture into a large piping bag fitted with a plain ½ inch nozzle. Twist the bag to seal. Pipe small, flattish mounds onto the prepared sheets, allowing room for spreading. Alternatively, place teaspoonfuls of meringue on the baking sheets. Sprinkle with the flaked almonds.

Bake two sheets at a time in the oven for 1 hour. Turn off the heat and leave in the oven until cool.

CHOCOLATE CREAM
Beat the cream until stiff. Fold in the tepid melted chocolate and flavor with confectioner's sugar and brandy or vanilla extract. Chill.

ASSEMBLY
Pair the meringues according to size. Sandwich each pair with the chocolate cream, place into small paper liners, and chill until ready to serve.

chapter eleven

THE FROSTING ON THE CAKE

Frostings, fillings, and glazes are the components that hold cakes together.

A glossy glaze or fluffy butter frosting can transform a plain cake; fillings, frostings,

and decorative elements bring out the best in special-occasion cakes and also hide

any flaws. It is these finishing touches that often make a cake memorable.

FROSTING BASICS

Whether you are adding a simple frosting to a plain cake, or lavishly decorating a special-occasion torte, preparing the cake properly beforehand will ensure a good result.

PREPARING CAKES FOR DECORATION

Cakes should be frosted only when they are completely cooled, or the frosting will melt and slide off the cake.

Position a cardboard cake board under the cake before it is frosted or glazed; this prevents the frosting or glaze from 'cracking' when the cake is transferred to a serving plate. To minimize mess when working with a runny frosting or glaze, position the cake on a wire rack over a baking sheet or roasting pan to catch drips.

If the top of the cake has cracked during baking, turn the cake upside down before frosting, to give a good base to work with.

Some recipes will call for the surface of the cake to be lightly brushed with a sugar syrup or jam glaze (see page 219) before it is frosted or filled. This adds flavor and moisture to the cake and also ensures that the filling or frosting adheres to its surface.

To obtain even layers when slicing cakes horizontally before filling them, use a ruler to measure the side of the cake vertically. Divide its height by the required number of layers, and mark each division with a toothpick. Proceed thus at intervals all around the cake, then, using a long-bladed sharp knife, slice the cake into layers using the toothpicks to guide you.

WORKING WITH FROSTINGS AND GLAZES

There is some overlap between frostings and glazes. Frostings have a basis of confectioner's sugar. They may also contain various other ingredients, such as butter, milk, eggs, water, and flavorings. Frostings may be cooked or uncooked, and should be soft enough to spread easily, yet thick enough to adhere to the cake. For frostings containing chocolate, especially ganache, use the best-quality chocolate to ensure that the mixture flows well and has high sheen.

Glazes tend to be thinner, pourable mixtures that are smooth and shiny once set. Some glazes contain confectioner's sugar; others may be made wholly or partially of chocolate.

Some frosting mixtures, such as buttercream, can also be used to fill a cake. Buttercream is also used to thinly coat the surface of, for example, wedding cakes, before they are frosted or glazed. The buttercream coating prevents crumbs from marring the final frosting, and in the case of chocolate cakes also acts as an 'undercoat' to prevent the dark color of the cake showing through, especially when using white chocolate frostings or ganache.

When making a glaze from chocolate and cream, always add the hot cream to the chocolate, rather than the chocolate to the cream; this prevents the glaze from splitting.

Do not over-stir decorative glazes; instead, stir gently using a rubber spatula. This will help prevent the incorporation of air bubbles. To ensure the glaze stays shiny, cakes should be at room temperature before they are glazed and not refrigerated afterwards. Adding a few drops of glycerin or an alcohol such as brandy to a glaze will provide a high sheen.

Unless otherwise stated, all the frostings in this book require pure confectioner's sugar, rather than confectioner's sugar mixture, which has cornflour added to prevent clumping. Pure confectioner's sugar should always be sifted before use; if it contains large lumps, these may be broken up in a food processor before sifting.

SLICING CAKES FOR SERVING

For a neat, clean cut, use a sharp knife with a long blade. Dip the knife in a jug of boiling water, then dry the knife. You may have to repeat this for each slice, depending on the density of the cake or dessert, and the amount of chocolate it contains.

SYRUPS AND GLAZES

Sugar syrups and jam-based glazes are used to add flavor and moisture, and to ensure that cream or mousse fillings do not separate from the cake when it is being assembled and served.

SUGAR SYRUP

MAKES ABOUT 1 CUP

³/₄ cup water ▪
3¹/₂ oz sugar ▪
3 tablespoons liqueur or fruit juice ▪

Heat the water and sugar in a small saucepan and bring to a boil, stirring constantly. Remove from the heat and allow to cool. Stir in the liqueur or fruit juice.

Brush the syrup onto the surface of the cake before filling or frosting it. Store in a sealed container in the refrigerator for up to 1 month.

RUM SYRUP

MAKES ABOUT 1 CUP

3 fl oz water ▪
3¹/₄ oz sugar ▪
3 fl oz dark rum ▪

Combine the water and sugar in a small saucepan. Bring to the boil and cook until the sugar is completely dissolved, stirring occasionally. Cool and stir in the rum. Refrigerate until required.

Brush the syrup onto the surface of the cake before filling or frosting it.

NOTE Brandy, orange liqueur, or another liqueur of your choice may replace the rum.

APRICOT GLAZE

MAKES ABOUT 1 CUP

1 cup apricot jam ▪
¹/₄ cup water ▪

Heat the apricot jam and water in a small heavy-based saucepan until boiling. Pass through a fine strainer.

If more water is required to adjust the consistency, the glaze must be re-boiled before use. The glaze should always be at boiling point when used, to ensure that it sets well.

Brush the glaze onto the surface of the cake before filling or frosting it.

Tips
▪ The glaze may be flavored with brandy if desired.
▪ Store in a sealed container in the refrigerator for 2–3 days, or up to 1 month if the glaze is flavored with alcohol.
▪ Raspberry and strawberry jams may be used in the same way, to make a red glaze.

FILLINGS, FROSTINGS AND CHOCOLATE GLAZES

Some mixtures, such as buttercream, can be used to both fill and frost the cake; or fill the cake with whipped cream or a mousse filling and coat with the frosting or glaze of your choice.

CHOCOLATE BUTTERCREAM

SUFFICIENT TO FILL AND FROST ONE 9 INCH CAKE

2 large eggs ■
¼ cup superfine sugar ■
1 scant cup white sugar ■
1½ tablespoons liquid glucose ■
1⅔ cups unsalted butter, chopped, at room temperature ■
1⅓ cups chopped dark chocolate, melted and cooled ■

Using an electric mixer, whisk the eggs and superfine sugar for about 2 minutes, or until thick and pale.

Meanwhile, put the white sugar and 5 fl oz water in a saucepan and bring to a boil while stirring and brushing down the sides of the pan with a wet pastry brush to prevent crystals from forming. Add the glucose and boil, without stirring, until the mixture reaches 239–242.5°F (soft-ball stage) on a sugar thermometer.

While continuing to whisk the egg mixture, gradually add the hot syrup (to prevent spatters, avoid pouring it on the whisk). Continue beating until the mixture is tepid.

Gradually beat in the butter, piece by piece, until the mixture is smooth.

Add the cooled melted chocolate and beat lightly until combined. Do not overbeat.

Chill until the mixture is of spreading consistency, stirring occasionally.

NOTE This is a light, smooth, glossy mixture with a delicate flavor; it is ideal for a special-occasion cake. Adjust the quantity if using it for a wedding cake.

Tip
■ This frosting is best made the day before use. It will keep for several days in the refrigerator.

VARIATION
1 tablespoon freshly brewed strong coffee or liqueur may be added for additional flavor.

WHITE CHOCOLATE MERINGUE BUTTERCREAM

TO MAKE 10 CUPS: SUFFICIENT TO FROST FOUR 9 INCH CAKES, OR TO FILL AND FROST TWO 9 INCH CAKES

4⅓ cups superfine sugar ▪
8–10 large egg whites ▪
5 cups unsalted butter, cut into pieces ▪
(use French white butter if available)
3½ cups chopped white chocolate, melted ▪

TO MAKE 4 CUPS: SUFFICIENT TO FILL AND FROST ONE 10 INCH CAKE

2¼ cups caster (superfine) sugar ▪
4 large egg whites ▪
2 cups unsalted butter, cut into pieces ▪
(use French white butter if available)
1¾ cups chopped white chocolate, melted ▪

Place the sugar and egg whites in the heatproof bowl of an electric mixer and place over a saucepan of simmering water. Beat for 3–5 minutes, until the mixture is warm and the sugar has dissolved. Remove from the heat.

Using the electric mixer with a whisk attachment, beat on high speed until stiff peaks form. Continue beating on medium speed for 10–15 minutes, until the mixture has cooled.

Still beating on medium speed, add the butter, one piece at a time, beating until well blended. Scrape down the sides of the bowl from time to time.

Beating at high speed, add the tepid melted chocolate.

Use immediately, or spoon into a sealed container and refrigerate for up to 1 week. Allow to return to room temperature before using.

NOTE This beautiful soft buttercream has a delicate flavor, and is ideal for covering wedding cakes, as its glossy, velvet-smooth finish is most attractive. The cake must be refrigerated for 2–3 hours before serving. Unfortunately, this buttercream does not hold up well in hot, humid conditions.

VARIATIONS
DARK CHOCOLATE
Use 3⅓ cups chopped dark chocolate.

MILK CHOCOLATE
Use 3⅓ cups chopped milk chocolate.

CHOCOLATE GANACHE CREAM

SUFFICIENT TO FILL AND FROST ONE 12 INCH
CAKE OR TWO 8 INCH CAKES

5⅓ cups chopped dark chocolate ▪
4 cups whipping cream ▪
2 tablespoons plus 1 teaspoon liquid glucose ▪

Put the chocolate in a heatproof bowl over hot water and melt it to 104°F on a sugar thermometer.

Combine the cream and liquid glucose in a saucepan and bring to a boil. Remove from the heat.

Add the boiled cream to the melted chocolate and stir thoroughly until smooth. Chill for about 2 hours.

Using an electric mixer, beat the chilled mixture for 3–5 minutes, or until thickened. Do not overwhip. The ganache will keep in an airtight container in the freezer for up to 6 months.

Tip
▪ Use a hot dry spoon to measure liquid glucose.

CHOCOLATE PASTRY CREAM

MAKES ABOUT 24 FL OZ: SUFFICIENT TO FILL
ONE 9½–10½ INCH PASTRY SHELL

4 large egg yolks ▪
¼ cup superfine sugar ▪
2 tablespoons all-purpose flour, sifted ▪
7 fl oz whole milk ▪
1¼ cups cream ▪
⅔ cup chopped dark or milk chocolate ▪

Using an electric mixer, beat the egg yolks with the sugar and flour for about 3 minutes, until the mixture is pale and thickened.

Heat the milk and cream in a saucepan until just boiling and pour over the egg-yolk mixture. Return the mixture to the saucepan, place over low heat, and stir until boiling. Gently cook the custard, stirring, for 2 minutes.

Add the chocolate and leave for 2 minutes to melt. Stir, then allow to cool, stirring occasionally to prevent a skin forming.

Cover with plastic wrap, pressing it onto the surface. Refrigerate until required.

This filling is suitable for fresh fruit tarts and cream puffs.

DARK CHOCOLATE MOUSSE FILLING

MAKES 4 CUPS

2 large eggs ■
3 large egg yolks ■
½ cup sugar ■
2⅓ cups chopped dark chocolate, ■
melted and cooled to tepid
2 cups whipping cream ■

Beat the eggs and egg yolks in the bowl of an electric mixer for 2–3 minutes, or until thickened.

Meanwhile, heat the sugar with 3 tablespoons water in a small saucepan until it reaches 235°F (soft-ball stage) on a sugar thermometer. While continuing to whisk the egg mixture, gradually add the hot syrup (to prevent spatters, avoid pouring it on the beaters). Whisk until tepid and thickened.

Gently fold the tepid melted chocolate into the egg mixture until thoroughly mixed. Whip the cream to soft peaks and fold in using a rubber spatula.

NOTE If calculating how much mousse filling is needed for cakes of various sizes, use the following as a guide. These quantities are for one layer of filling: adjust for cakes with more layers.

- For an 8 inch cake: ¾ cup
- For a 9 inch cake:1 cup
- For a 10 inch cake: 1¼ cups
- For a 12 inch cake: 1¾ cups
- For a 15 inch cake: 2½ cups

Tips
- If a lighter mousse is required, whip the cream to soft peaks before folding it into the chocolate mixture.
- If making this recipe in hot or humid weather, increase the chocolate content to 1⅔ cups and decrease the cream to 1½ cups. The extra chocolate stabilizes the mixture due to its fat content.

CHOCOLATE MOUSSE FILLING

SUFFICIENT TO FILL ONE 8–8 1/2 INCH CAKE

4 1/2 oz dark, milk or white chocolate ▪
1 tablespoon unsalted butter ▪
4 large eggs, separated ▪

Melt the chocolate in a heatproof bowl over hot water. Add the butter, then work in the egg yolks one at a time using a wooden spoon or rubber spatula. Remove from the heat.

Using clean beaters, whisk the egg whites in a clean, dry bowl until stiff peaks form, then fold the egg whites through the chocolate mixture in two additions.

Cover and refrigerate until ready to use.

NOTE This is a delicate, creamy filling that is suitable for meringues, genoise sponge cakes and dessert cakes.

WHITE CHOCOLATE MOUSSE FILLING

MAKES 4 CUPS

2 teaspoons powdered gelatin ▪
2 1/3 cups chopped white chocolate ▪
29 fl oz whipping cream ▪

In a small bowl, soak the gelatin in 2 tablespoons water, then heat gently over a bowl of hot water or in the microwave to dissolve.

Melt the white chocolate in a heatproof bowl over hot water and stir until smooth.

Heat 1 3/4 cups of the cream in a heavy-based saucepan and bring gently to a boil. Remove from the heat, then add the gelatin and melted chocolate. Stir to mix thoroughly, then allow to cool, stirring occasionally.

Beat the remaining cream until stiff peaks form.

Using a rubber spatula, fold the whipped cream into the chocolate mixture until combined.

NOTE This delicate, frothy mousse is suitable for use in fruit-filled layer cakes. Alternatively, it may be served on its own as a dessert, either in individual bowls or buffet-style in a large bowl, and accompanied with seasonal fruits and delicate sweet cookies.

CHOCOLATE BUTTER FROSTING

SUFFICIENT TO FROST ONE 8 INCH CAKE

1½ tablespoons unsalted butter, cubed, ∎
at room temperature
⅔ cup chopped dark chocolate, melted ∎
1 tablespoon rum or freshly brewed espresso coffee (optional) ∎

Add the butter to the melted chocolate and stir until the butter is melted and the mixture is smooth. Add the rum or coffee, if using. Allow to cool until the mixture is of a spreadable consistency.

GLOSSY CHOCOLATE FROSTING

SUFFICIENT TO FROST ONE 8–9 INCH CAKE

¼ cup sugar ∎
1 cup chopped dark chocolate ∎
¼ cup unsalted butter, chilled and chopped ∎

Combine the sugar and ¼ cup water in a small saucepan over medium heat. Using a wooden spoon, stir until the sugar is dissolved and the mixture is boiling. Reduce the heat and boil for 2 minutes without stirring, brushing down the sides of the pan with a wet pastry brush to prevent crystals from forming. Remove from the heat. Add the chocolate and stir until smooth.

Allow to cool a little, then stir in the butter. Allow to stand until the mixture has thickened to a spreadable consistency. Pour over the cold cake and smooth with a spatula.

CHOCOLATE FROSTING

SUFFICIENT TO FILL AND FROST ONE 10 INCH CAKE

1⅔ cups finely chopped dark, milk or white chocolate ∎
1⅓ cups unsalted butter, at room temperature ∎
3⅓ cups pure confectioner's sugar ∎

Melt the chocolate in a heatproof bowl over a saucepan of hot water. Remove from the heat, stir until smooth and allow to cool to room temperature. Using an electric mixer, beat the butter until smooth, about 30 seconds. Add the sifted confectioner's sugar and beat until pale and creamy.

Beat in the melted chocolate. Continue beating until thoroughly mixed, but do not overbeat, as the mixture may separate.

EASY CHOCOLATE GLAZE

SUFFICIENT TO FROST ONE 8–9 INCH CAKE

½ cup whipping cream ▪
2 cups finely chopped dark chocolate ▪

Heat the cream in a small saucepan until just boiling. Remove from the heat and add the chocolate, stirring until all the chocolate has melted and the mixture is smooth.

Set aside to cool slightly until it reaches a coating consistency, stirring occasionally. Pour the glaze over the top of the cake and smooth with a metal spatula.

RICH CHOCOLATE GLAZE

SUFFICIENT TO FROST ONE 8–9 INCH CAKE

2 cups chopped dark, milk or white chocolate ▪
½ cup whipping cream ▪
2 teaspoons liquid glucose or light corn syrup ▪
A few drops of alcohol, such as brandy (optional, ▪
but it will help to give a high-gloss finish to the glaze)

Melt the chocolate in a heatproof bowl over a saucepan of hot water. Heat the cream and glucose in a small saucepan until just boiling. Pour the cream mixture over the chocolate and stir gently to combine. Set aside to cool slightly, until the mixture reaches a coating consistency.

Set the cake on a wire cake rack placed over a baking sheet to catch any excess glaze. Pour the glaze over the cake, allowing the glaze to run down the sides of the cake to cover it. To spread the glaze, use a spatula dipped in hot water then dried.

NOTE To frost a 10-inch cake, make 1½ quantities.

WHITE SATIN GLAZE

SUFFICIENT TO FROST ONE 8 INCH CAKE

¼ cup whipping cream ▪
1 teaspoon light corn syrup ▪
1 cup chopped white chocolate, melted ▪

In a small saucepan over low–medium heat, bring the cream and corn syrup just to boiling point. Pour the hot cream over the melted chocolate. Stir gently, then refrigerate, stirring occasionally, until the mixture has thickened to a spreadable consistency.

THE MAGIC OF GANACHE

For lovers of chocolate and cream, ganache is not only a staple element when cooking with chocolate, it is the ideal way to indulge in two of life's pleasures at the same time.

Best known as the classic filling or base for truffles, ganache is also used as a filling or glaze on cakes and is the basis of many chocolate tarts, desserts, soufflés, and ice creams.

Creating a luscious melt-in-the-mouth ganache is not complicated, provided the right ingredients are used. For best results, use pouring or whipping cream with a fat content of 35 per cent, and a good-quality chocolate—the smoother the chocolate, the smoother the ganache. The mixture will keep, refrigerated in a sealed container, for up to 10 days as long as the cream is heated to boiling point and strict hygiene standards are followed.

INGREDIENTS AND QUANTITIES

Ganache is prepared in varying consistencies depending on its intended use. The higher the ratio of chocolate to cream, the thicker the result. The method is the same whatever the consistency used.

HEAVY GANACHE (MAKES 1⅓ CUPS)
This is used for cutting out shapes.

- 3½ fl oz whipping cream
- 1⅔ cups chopped dark chocolate OR 1¼ cups chopped milk chocolate OR 2 cups chopped white chocolate

MEDIUM GANACHE (MAKES 1¼ CUPS)
This light, melt-in-the-mouth ganache is ideal for truffles and other chocolate specialities.

- 3½ fl oz whipping cream
- 1¼ cups chopped dark chocolate OR 1½ cups chopped milk chocolate OR 1¾ cups chopped white chocolate

SOFT GANACHE (MAKES 1 CUP)
Used for pipings, fillings, and glazes.

- 3½ fl oz whipping cream
- 1 cup chopped dark chocolate OR 1 cup chopped milk chocolate OR 1¼ cups chopped white chocolate

METHODS FOR MAKING GANACHE

TRADITIONAL METHOD
Finely chop or grate the chocolate (this can be done in a food processor) and place it in a medium heatproof bowl.

Bring the cream just to a boil in a heavy-based saucepan over low heat. Remove from the heat.

Add the hot cream to the finely chopped chocolate, allow to stand for 2 minutes, then stir gently until smooth. Allow to cool, depending on the use to which it is being put.

ALTERNATIVE METHOD
Melt the chocolate in a bowl over hot water.

Bring the cream just to a boil in a heavy-based saucepan over low heat. Remove from the heat.

Pour the melted chocolate into the hot cream and stir gently until combined. Allow to cool to room temperature, then stir gently.

BUTTER GANACHE
A delicate buttery ganache for pipings, fillings, and glazes.

- ½ cup unsalted butter, at room temperature
- 12 fl oz whipping cream
- 3 cups chopped dark chocolate, melted

Work the butter into a paste using a wooden spoon.

Bring the cream just to a boil in a heavy-based saucepan over low heat. Remove from the heat.

Add the melted chocolate and stir until smooth.

Allow to cool for 5 minutes, then stir in the creamed butter a tablespoon at a time. Allow to cool to room temperature or to a spreadable consistency (depending on the use to which it is being put) before using.

ADDING FLAVORS

Various flavors produce excellent results when added directly to the cream. Coffee, tea, vanilla bean, and spices are best infused into the cream while cooking and strained out before the cream is poured over the chocolate.

Alcohol should be added at the very end so that the flavor does not evaporate due to heat.

If adding a liquid flavoring (such as alcohol or espresso coffee) to the ganache, reduce the volume of cream by the amount of liquid that you are adding.

Vanilla   For a fresh vanilla flavor, infuse a 2 inch piece of vanilla pod in the cream. Heat the cream, then remove the pod before adding the cream to the grated chocolate.

Liqueurs   Liqueurs such as Grand Marnier, rum, cassis, or Kahlúa can be added to the ganache while it is warm (but not hot).

Coffee   Instant coffee granules or fresh espresso coffee may be added to the ganache while it is warm.

Nuts   Chopped plain or toasted nuts add texture and flavor to ganache. Add them to the finished ganache.

Praline   Praline (see page 112) made with the nuts of your choice, then finely crushed, adds a nutty crunch to fillings.

TIPS AND TROUBLESHOOTING

- Before coating a cake with a ganache glaze, brush the cake with hot sieved apricot jam and alcohol-infused sugar syrup (see page 219).

- To prevent crystallization and streaking, add two teaspoons of liquid glucose to the cream when heating.

- Once the cream is added to the chocolate, the ganache may separate (also known as 'splitting' or 'breaking'). To remedy this, gradually add a little boiled cream or spirit alcohol (such as brandy) to the center of the mixture and stir gently until the ganache re-emulsifies and is smooth.

- If making a ganache glaze, avoid vigorous stirring, as this will aerate the mixture. Stir with a rubber spatula.

- If making a ganache filling or glaze, prepare the mixture the day before use and allow it to stand overnight to mature. Then, if using it as a glaze, warm the mixture very gently over hot water to soften it before use. If using it as a filling, aerate the chilled mixture with an electric mixer on high speed until pale and fluffy; do not overbeat.

CHOCOLATE GANACHE GLAZE

MAKES ABOUT 3 CUPS: SUFFICIENT TO FROST ONE 10 INCH CAKE

1⅓ cups whipping cream ■
1⅔ cups chopped dark chocolate, melted ■

VARIATION
BUTTER GLAZE
Make the ganache as above. When the mixture is smooth, stir in ¾ cup room-temperature unsalted butter, 1 tablespoon at a time, making sure each piece has been fully incorporated before adding more. This produces a shiny, dark glaze that spreads easily.

Bring the cream just to a boil in a small saucepan over low heat.

Pour the hot cream over the melted chocolate and stir using a rubber spatula until the mixture is smooth. Allow to cool to a pouring consistency. (Note that as the ganache cools, it will thicken and become stiff. If you leave it so long that it becomes too cool and sets, and you need to thin the glaze, put it over a saucepan of hot water, off the heat.)

Set the cake on a wire cake rack placed over a baking sheet to catch any excess glaze, then pour the glaze over the cake.

Tip
■ Do not use a whisk to beat the glaze, as it aerates the mixture, causing air bubbles to form and marring the smooth appearance.

GANACHE GLAZE FOR CHILLED CAKES

SUFFICIENT TO COVER ONE 8–9½ INCH CAKE

1 teaspoon powdered gelatin ■
½ cup milk ■
2 tablespoons liquid glucose ■
1⅔ cups chopped dark chocolate, melted ■

Soak the gelatin in 1 tablespoon water. Heat gently over a bowl of hot water or in the microwave oven to dissolve the gelatin.

Bring the milk and glucose to a boil in a saucepan. Remove from the heat. Add the gelatin and melted chocolate, and stir well. Strain and use immediately, or allow to cool to room temperature before coating the cake.

If making ahead, cover the ganache glaze with plastic wrap pressed onto the surface to prevent a skin forming and refrigerate.

NOTE This glaze is suitable for chilled cakes and desserts that are perishable. The item to be glazed must be well chilled before glazing, and refrigerated immediately afterwards to prevent the glaze from streaking. The inclusion of glucose gives the glaze elasticity. This mixture is best stored in the freezer. When required, it can be reheated in the microwave in short bursts at medium heat.

CHOCOLATE SAUCES

The addition of a delicious chocolate sauce and some ice cream or whipped cream is enough to transform a plain cake into a dessert.

MARSHMALLOW CHOCOLATE SAUCE

MAKES 1⅓ CUPS

½ cup whipping cream ▪
1 cup white marshmallows ▪
1⅓ cups chopped dark chocolate ▪

Put all the ingredients in a small saucepan and heat gently, stirring with a wooden spoon, until melted and smooth.

Spoon over ice cream, banana splits, stewed fruit, or milk drinks.

WHITE CHOCOLATE SAUCE

MAKES 2 CUPS

2 cups chopped white chocolate ▪
7 fl oz whipping cream ▪
1½ tablespoons pure confectioner's sugar, sifted ▪
1 tablespoon light corn syrup ▪
2–4 tablespoons brandy or orange liqueur ▪

Put the chocolate, cream, and confectioner's sugar in a heatproof bowl over hot water and allow to melt without stirring.

Remove from the heat, stir in the corn syrup, and allow to cool.

Add the brandy or liqueur to taste, stir and serve.

DARK CHOCOLATE SAUCE

MAKES 2 CUPS

1 cup whipping cream ▪
¾–1⅓ cups chopped dark chocolate ▪
¼ cup unsalted butter, at room temperature ▪
1–2 tablespoons pure confectioner's sugar, sifted ▪

Bring the cream just to a boil in a small saucepan. Remove from the heat. Add the chopped chocolate, allow to stand for 5 minutes, then add the butter and confectioner's sugar and stir until smooth.

Serve with ice cream, cake, or desserts and fruits.

FRUIT SAUCES

*Fruit sauces, as well as being delightfully sweet and tangy,
add a cheerful burst of bright color to chocolate desserts and cakes.*

CHERRY SAUCE

MAKES 2 CUPS

2½ cups fresh cherries, pitted ▪
¼ cup sugar ▪
Pinch of ground cinnamon ▪
1 tablespoon arrowroot or cornstarch ▪
2 tablespoons water or fresh lemon juice ▪

Combine the cherries, sugar, and cinnamon in a saucepan, cover and cook gently until the cherries yield up their juice. Bring to a boil.

Blend the arrowroot or cornstrarch with the water or lemon juice and stir into the boiling cherries. Return to a boil, then remove from the heat and allow to cool.

VARIATION

If cherries are not in season, canned pitted black cherries can replace them.

ORANGE SAUCE

MAKES 1½ CUPS

7 fl oz fresh orange juice ▪
2 teaspoons orange zest ▪
Sugar to taste ▪
2 tablespoons orange liqueur, such as Grand Marnier ▪
1 tablespoon unsalted butter ▪

Bring the orange juice, zest, and sugar to a boil in a small heavy-based saucepan. Simmer, stirring, until the sugar is dissolved.

Remove from the heat. Add the liqueur, whisk in the butter, and chill until ready to serve. Strain if desired.

Tip
▪ Serve with White Chocolate Mousse.

APRICOT SAUCE

MAKES 2 CUPS

1 lb 2 oz fresh apricots, pitted and puréed ▪
⅓ cup lightly packed soft brown sugar ▪
1 tablespoon lemon juice ▪

Put the apricot purée in a saucepan with the sugar and lemon juice. Bring to a boil, then immediately cool over ice cubes to prevent darkening of the fruit.

Tip
▪ Frozen pulp may be used.

BERRY SAUCE

MAKES 2½ CUPS

3½ cups fresh strawberries, raspberries, ◼
blackberries and/or blueberries
1–2 teaspoons pure confectioner's sugar (optional) ◼
Juice of 1 lemon ◼
Kirsch, brandy or orange liqueur, to taste (optional) ◼

Place the berries in a blender or food processor and purée until smooth, then strain through a sieve if desired. Add confectioner's sugar and lemon juice to taste and the liqueur, if using. Refrigerate until ready to serve. The sauce will keep, refrigerated, for up to 3 days.

PASSIONFRUIT SAUCE

MAKES 1½–2 CUPS

Pulp of 6 fresh large passionfruit ◼
Juice of 1 medium orange ◼
1 tablespoon superfine sugar ◼
1 teaspoon cornstarch, blended with ◼
3 tablespoons water

Combine the passionfruit pulp, orange juice, and sugar in a small saucepan. Stir over low heat and bring to a boil.

Stir in the blended cornstarch, and continue stirring until the mixture thickens. Allow to cool. Strain to remove the seeds if desired.

MANGO SAUCE

MAKES 2 CUPS

½ cup peeled and chopped ripe mango ◼
1 orange, peeled, seeded, and chopped ◼
2 teaspoons fresh lime or lemon juice ◼
1–2 teaspoons sugar, to taste ◼

Place the mango, orange juice, and lemon juice in a blender or food processor and blend to a purée. Add sugar to taste if desired.

KIWIFRUIT SAUCE

MAKES 1½–2 CUPS

5 kiwifruit, peeled and chopped ◼
2–3 teaspoons sugar ◼
½ cup water ◼

Blend the fruit to a purée in a blender or food processor. Add the sugar and enough water to give a sauce-like consistency. Strain through a fine sieve to remove the seeds.

CHOCOLATE SPECIAL EFFECTS

Chocolate special effects can be used to embellish large cakes, cupcakes, petits fours, desserts, and ice creams. Such decorations can be as simple as chopped or grated chocolate, or as elaborate as piping or shapes molded from chocolate plastic.

Use tempered couverture chocolate for maximum impact when making chocolate decorations. Compound chocolate can be used successfully, but it does not have the richness or depth of flavor of couverture, and is gritty and very sweet. However, it is suitable for some applications; children, especially, are likely to neither know nor care if the decorations on their cake are made from compound chocolate rather than couverture.

When working with chocolate decorations, wear cotton gloves to prevent the chocolate from melting or showing fingerprints when you touch it.

SIMPLE DECORATIVE EFFECTS

UNSWEETENED COCOA POWDER
Sifted unsweetened cocoa powder can be used as decorative coating for, for example, truffles. To sift, spoon the powder into a fine-meshed metal sieve held over a bowl. Tap the sides of the sieve firmly with your hand until the powder has fallen through. Any lumps may be crushed and pushed through with the back of a spoon. For a sweeter powder, combine the cocoa with confectioner's sugar and sift them together.

CHOPPED CHOCOLATE
Break the chocolate into small pieces and place on a chopping board. Hold a cook's knife by the handle and the tip of the blade and chop the chocolate into pieces of the desired size.

GRATING CHOCOLATE
Chill the chocolate in the refrigerator for about 15 minutes (warm chocolate clogs the grater). Rest one side of the grater on a plate to catch the chocolate as you grate. If the chocolate needs to be weighed, grate it onto a piece of parchment paper so that it can easily be placed on the scales. Grating tends to create static magnetism in the chocolate, so it may be necessary to brush down the grater with a soft brush. Avoid touching the grated chocolate with your fingers, as the warmth of your hands will melt it.

MAKING CHOCOLATE CURLS (THE EASY WAY)
Hold a block of room-temperature chocolate over a plate and draw the blade of a vegetable peeler towards you along the long edge of the block. This results in long decorative curls.

CHOCOLATE SHAPES AND PIPING

MAKING CHOCOLATE ROLLS
Pour melted chocolate onto a marble slab if you have one, or a large smooth glass tile or clean work surface. Use a flexible metal spatula to spread the chocolate to a thickness of 1/8 inch or less. Allow the chocolate to cool and harden.

Push a stiff, wide-bladed tool, such as a clean paint scraper, under the chocolate, using a continuous motion to create the chocolate rolls.

DECORATIVE CHOCOLATE LEAVES
- Camellia leaves, rose leaves, or prunus leaves
- 2/3 cup chopped dark, white or milk chocolate, melted

Ensure the leaves are clean, dry and unsprayed. Rub with a pad of cotton wool to polish them, leaving the stalks intact.

Dip the underside of the leaves in melted chocolate and remove any excess by brushing the leaf against the rim of the bowl. (A small teaspoon or paintbrush may also be used to coat the leaves.) Put the leaves on parchment paper on a baking sheet and refrigerate until set. When set, ease the chocolate from the leaves. Work from the stem end to the tip.

CUTTING DECORATIVE SHAPES
Use a marble tile, or line a baking sheet with parchment paper or foil. Pour in melted chocolate to a depth of 1/4 inch. Allow the chocolate to set, then gently turn out on to a clean work surface. Remove the paper or foil. Using a sharp knife or fancy cutters, cut out desired shapes.

PIPING SHAPES AND ILLUSTRATIONS
Melt 3/4 cup chopped dark chocolate and add 2 drops glycerin (available from pharmacies). Stir to amalgamate. Fill a piping bag made from parchment paper, or use a plastic bag, snipping off the corner. Pipe directly onto greaseproof paper over illustrations drawn onto parchment paper. In this way you obtain uniform shape and size. Allow to set, then remove from the greaseproof paper using the point of a sharp knife.

PIPING DIRECTLY ONTO THE CAKE

Melt 3/4 cup dark chocolate and add 2 drops glycerin (available from pharmacies). Stir, then spoon the chocolate into a piping bag fitted with a metal nozzle, making sure the bag is no more than two-thirds full. Pipe the chocolate onto the cake.

To make a quick and easy piping bag, put chopped chocolate in a small microwave-safe plastic bag. Heat gently to melt the chocolate. Push the melted chocolate to one corner of the bag and seal the open end to stop the chocolate escaping. Snip the corner from the bag and pipe as desired. Discard the bag after use.

FEATHERING CHOCOLATE

This creates a pretty effect on the surface of a cake or dessert. Two different colors of chocolate are required. First, glaze the cake or dessert with dark or milk chocolate; do not allow it to set. Then melt a small amount of lighter-colored chocolate and place in a piping bag or small plastic bag with the corner snipped off. Pipe parallel lines about 1/2 inch apart across the cake (begin and end each stripe off the surface of the cake so that there will be no loops or splodges on the sides of the cake). Working quickly, before the chocolate sets, use the tip of a toothpick or fine skewer to pull across the lines at right angles at 1 inch intervals from left to right. Next, pull the toothpick or skewer from right to left between each of the previous pulls, thus creating a feathered effect.

MARBLING CHOCOLATE

This creates a more random pattern than feathering. Glaze the cake with melted dark or milk chocolate, then melt a small amount of lighter-colored chocolate and place it in a piping bag or small plastic bag with the corner snipped off. Use it to streak the surface of the cake in a series of curves. Then, with the point of a toothpick or fine skewer, draw a series of arcs or lines across the streaks.

WORKING WITH ACETATE

The use of acetate (plastic) sheets enables many decorative finishes to be achieved to add glamor to chocolate cakes and desserts. As acetate is flexible and smooth, the chocolate comes away from it easily, and with an enhanced sheen. The acetate sheets can be washed and re-used. Avoid scratching them, as the scratches will show on the chocolate.

Observe the following when working with acetate:

- Use tempered couverture chocolate.
- Ensure the acetate sheets are clean and dry.
- Do not work chocolate directly on the acetate.
- Use a spatula for spreading, working quickly; speed is essential for success.
- Allow the spread chocolate on the acetate sheet to stand at room temperature until set to the touch.
- Refrigerate for 5–10 minutes.
- Do not remove the acetate straight away; instead, leave at room temperature for up to one day if possible.

CHOCOLATE SHEETS

Sheets of chocolate of varying appearance can be achieved by dusting a plastic sheet with sifted unsweetened cocoa powder. Then spread a thin layer of white chocolate on top. To achieve a marble effect, mix two tones of chocolate. If you need to lift and move the sheet, is important to do so while the chocolate is still wet.

USING TEMPERED COCOA BUTTER

Tempered cocoa butter can be colored with cake decorating colors and applied to acetate in the following ways:

- Using a stiff pastry brush, dot it on to achieve a stipple effect
- Apply it with a small sponge paint roller
- Apply droplets of cocoa butter
- Brush it on
- Pour it on in streaks using a rubber spatula.

Tempered milk, dark, or white chocolate is then spread thinly over the design and the chocolate left to set. Once set, the chocolate will come away from the acetate naturally.

To temper cocoa butter, chop it very finely and add sieved, oil-based food coloring powder, if desired, before melting. Melt slowly in a microwave-safe bowl, for 30 seconds at a time, on low power, without heating it above 88°F. Take it back to 80°F.

If small crystals (lumps) are still present, do not re-heat the cocoa butter again in the microwave. Instead, use a hair dryer and a thermometer.

MAKING CHOCOLATE RIBBONS, BOWS, AND WRAPS

To make a chocolate band to wrap around the outside of a cake, cut a strip of acetate the same depth as the cake and about 1/2 inch longer than its circumference (this overlap is needed to allow for shrinkage in the chocolate.) Spread tempered chocolate on the acetate to a thickness of 1/8 inch or less, and wrap the band around the cake, acetate side out, and secure with a paper clip. Allow to set until the chocolate comes away from the acetate of its own accord, then remove the clip and carefully peel away the acetate.

To make chocolate ribbons and bows, spread tempered chocolate on strip(s) of acetate (allow one strip for the ribbon, plus one for each loop of the bow). Run your fingers along either side of the strip to ensure the edge is clear of chocolate. Fold back the acetate to form a loop and secure with a paper clip. Allow to stand for 1 day, then release the clip, peel off the acetate and position the loops to form a decorative bow. Secure all the components together with a little melted chocolate.

WORKING WITH CHOCOLATE PLASTIC

Chocolate plastic is an edible modelling paste used for many decorative techniques. It is suitable for rolling out and wrapping around a cake, making flowers, leaves, ribbons, bows, and other three-dimensional decorations.

Decorations made of chocolate plastic dry very hard and can be made up to a month in advance. They need to breathe, however, so should not be stored in an airtight container; use a cardboard cake box instead. Avoid humidity, and never refrigerate them, as beads of moisture will form, spoiling the appearance.

If making white chocolate plastic, white compound chocolate gives the most reliable results. If making dark or milk chocolate plastic, couverture chocolate gives a far superior product for eating, although compound chocolate (compound coating) may be used if you prefer. Chocolate plastic should be stored at room temperature.

The following recipe is sufficient to decorate 2–3 cakes or desserts.

MAKING CHOCOLATE PLASTIC

- 4 cups chopped dark or milk couverture or compound chocolate, or white compound chocolate
- 2/3 cup light corn syrup (for dark chocolate plastic); OR 1/2 cup light corn syrup (for white chocolate plastic)

Melt the chocolate gently in a heatproof bowl over hot water. Pour the melted chocolate into the bowl of an electric mixer. Mixing on low speed, and using the paddle attachment, pour in the corn syrup and increase the speed for 50–60 seconds. Alternatively, mix with a rubber spatula. Scrape down the sides of the bowl. Pour or scrape the dough onto plastic wrap, seal and allow to firm at room temperature for 2 hours or overnight before working.

If the mixture becomes too firm, knead it in your hands for about 20 seconds and the dough will become pliable again; alternatively, microwave it on low power in 10-second pulses.

A crank-handled pasta machine can be used to roll the chocolate plastic into thin sheets before cutting out shapes. Use sifted unsweetened cocoa powder when rolling out the dough. Use the chocolate plastic to make ribbons, drapes, ruffles, bows, curls, and molded flowers and leaves. Allow to dry overnight before using to decorate the cake. Chocolate plastic will keep in an airtight container at room temperature for up to 1 month.

DECORATING WITH METALLIC LEAF

Gold and silver leaf are used for decorating exquisite cakes and confectionery. They are edible, and can be bought in art shops, cake decorating shops, specialty and Indian food stores. Store in an airtight container in a cool, dry cupboard; the leaf will keep indefinitely, although silver leaf will tarnish over time.

Metallic leaf is very fragile and extremely difficult to work with. Avoid working in a draft, as it can blow away. It collapses easily, so care must be taken when handling it. Hands must be dry, and metal implements avoided as they cause static magnetism. Disposable plastic tweezers are an excellent tool for handling metallic leaf. Use a dry spatula to gently separate the leaf from the interleaves of tissue paper. Apply the leaf to the surface to be decorated using plastic tweezers and a toothpick.

INDEX

Entries in **bold** type refer to photographs.

ACKNOWLEDGMENTS

I would like to thank all at Murdoch Books for the opportunity to realize my passion for chocolate. Special thanks to my editor, Janine Flew, for her dedication to this project; to Vivien Valk, for her creative and artistic design; to Kay Scarlett and Diana Hill, for their warm encouragement; and to the recipe testers, for their suggestions.

Thanks are due to Adrian and Adair Lander, for helping with the book proposal, and for the photography, and to Simon Bajada, for styling. Nick Malgieri and Loretta Sartori deserve a special mention for their professional encouragement and advice over the years, as do Wendy Hovey and Veronica Rickard, for typing recipes and sorting out my paperwork. Also, I wish to thank the many wonderful friends who have contributed to this book, among them June Blanchett, Linda Brushfield, Von Canty, Fernando Cappelluti of Brunetti, Chocolatier Australia, the Cipriani Family of Venice, Zoi Condos, Elaine González, Nola Heffernan, Sylvia Kliska, Tony Knox, Janet Lillie, Lucinda McCook, Jennifer Migliorelli, Rosemary Nutbeam, Patricia O'Donnell, Rosemary Portelli, Margo Stubbs, Beverley Sutherland-Smith, Kirsten Tibballs, and Peter Wilson.

Thanks, too, to Terri Mercieca, a true star, for her wonderful assistance during the long hours at the photoshoot, and most particularly to my husband, Peter, and sons, Andy and James, who have supported me every step of the way and helped with shopping, preparation, washing up, transporting equipment and, of course, with sampling and enjoying the chocolate treats.

text © 2007 by Maureen McKeon; photography © 2007 by Adrian Lander; design © 2007 by Murdoch Books

This 2008 edition published by Metro Books,
by arrangement with Murdoch Books.

Text: Maureen McKeon
Concept and design: Vivien Valk
Photographer: Adrian Lander
Stylist: Simon Bajada
Production: Monique Layt
Food preparation: Maureen McKeon and Terri Mercieca

Metro Books
122 Fifth Avenue
New York, NY 10011

ISBN-13: 978-1-4351-0507-2
ISBN-10: 1-4351-0507-9

Printed and bound in China

1 3 5 7 9 10 8 6 4 2

IMPORTANT: Those who might be at risk from the effects of salmonella poisoning (the elderly, pregnant women, young children, and those suffering from immune deficiency diseases) should consult their doctor with any concerns about eating raw eggs.

CONVERSION GUIDE: You may find cooking times vary depending on the oven you are using. For fan-forced ovens, as a general rule, set the oven temperature to 35°F lower than indicated in the recipe.